Heart & Soul Food

Tales of Food, Family, and Friends to nourish your heart and soul.

Peggy Browning

ISBN:152322794X
ISBN-13:978-1523227945

This book is dedicated to all the grandmothers, aunts, mothers, and sisters who have nourished us with their lovingly prepared food and expressed their care for us by adding the secret immeasurable ingredient to every dish they served.

It is also dedicated to my children: Matt, Ben, & Emily because they always ate whatever I put on the table with no complaints.

Chapter 1: The Secret Ingredient

"If you really want to make a friend, go to someone's house and eat with him… the people who give you their food give you their heart." - Cesar Chavez –

"I love the slow way of cooking. I like the country foods: the greens and the beans and the cornbreads and the biscuits. Not just for the taste, but because it infuses the house with an aroma that says 'You are welcome. You're going to have some good food. It's going to take some time. And once you eat it you won't want to leave.'"

- Maya Angelou

"The table is a meeting place, a gathering ground, the source of sustenance and nourishment, festivity, safety, and satisfaction. A person cooking is a person giving: Even the simplest food is a gift." -Laurie Colwin-

---

Grandchildren always remember how their grandparents made them feel. Many a grandmother has expressed her love with a pan of hot-from-the-oven biscuits, a jar of homemade jelly, and a glass of milk.

If you were to happen to drop in at the funeral of a Southern Grandmother, you might be surprised at the eulogy given. In fact, if you were not listening with your heart, you might think you were listening to the Special of the Day list at a restaurant.

I have attended many funerals where a grandson or

granddaughter was given the task of eulogizing their grandmother. Among the favorite memories, favorite foods are always mentioned. Bereaved grandchildren fondly memorialize the times spent at their grandmother's table, eating whatever her specialty was.

The fact is this: it's not about the food; it's about how they felt when gathered around their grandmother's table.

Each and every food prepared by a grandmother has the same secret ingredient. That ingredient is Love.

And it soothes and comforts your heart and soul.

The recipes in this book are favorites that have been served at family dinners, church suppers, and get-togethers with friends. They were concocted and shared long ago … before we called macaroni pasta and before we looked at the nutritional data on all things edible. There is no calorie count here.

These recipes were frugally designed using common ingredients that we all had in our kitchens and that we harvested from our gardens in the 1970s.

Love is the common ingredient in all the recipes featured here.

"Most of us have fond memories of food from our childhood. Whether it was our mom's homemade lasagna or a memorable chocolate birthday cake, food has a way of transporting us back to the past." Homaro Cantu

GRANDMA'S RECIPES

This has always puzzled me:
Just how much is a pinch?
These recipes of dear Grandma's
Surely are no cinch.

A "snip" of this, a "dab" of that,
A "lump" of something else…
Then "beat it for a little while",
Or, "stir until it melts."

I have to be a wizard
To decipher what she meant
By all these strange proportions
In her cookbook worn and bent.

How much nutmeg's in the doughnuts?
Grandma wouldn't flinch
As she said, with twinkling eyes,
"Oh, just about a pinch."

There must have been in her wise head
A measuring device
That told her just how much to use
Of sugar, salt, and spice.

Author: Unknown

Grandmas Chicken and Dumplings

Bless the food before us, the family beside us, and the love between us.

Amen

It was one of those days that required comfort food. It was cloudy, drizzly, and rainy…thank the Good Lord…and we needed something warm and rich to comfort us.

It was the perfect day to make Grandma's chicken and dumplings.

The only problem was that I don't really know how to make chicken and dumplings without using a can of biscuits.

You know the kind…the cheap ones that you pop open with a butter knife and then pinch off and throw into the pot of boiling chicken and broth. And I didn't have a can of biscuits.

But my youngest granddaughter and I needed something good to eat. We also needed something to occupy our time and our hands on this drizzly day.

So I pulled out an old cookbook that was put together by the ladies of the church I attended, figuring there would be one in there.

Sure enough, my friend Lucy had published her recipe for chicken and dumplings.

And they were the old-fashioned kind of dumplings…made with flour and shortening, salt and baking powder and milk. They were the kind my mother used to make, the ones she never used a recipe to make . The ones I didn't learn to make by watching her.

So I set the chicken to boiling in the pot and got the other ingredients for Lucy's recipe out of the cabinet. Then Baby Dear and I proceeded to make us some dumplings.

I measured the flour, the salt and the baking powder, then sifted them all together while Baby Dear sat in her high chair, contentedly tossing cereal in the floor and saying "Uh-oh" in her sweet little voice. I cut in the shortening with a potato masher because using a fork seemed like too much work. And that worked really well. I added milk and kneaded the dough in a bowl.

When I placed the dough on a sheet of waxed paper, I handed B.D. a handful of it and she "rolled it up and rolled it up" and threw it in the floor with the Cheerios. And she laughed and snorted and I laughed and snorted along with her.

I rolled out the dough with my mother's old rolling pin that's missing both handles. That rolling pin must have rolled out thousands of biscuits and pie crusts in her time.

When the dough was thin enough…about 1/8 of an inch…I cut it into strips and B.D. watched as I tossed each piece into the pot of hot broth.

Next I took all the ragged ends of the left over dough and rolled them in sugar and cinnamon. Then I placed them on a cookie sheet and put them in the oven, to bake a special treat for my little helper…just like my mother used to do for me.

When they were baked, B.D. and I shared the little bits of sugary dough while we waited for the dumplings to cook.

When the dumplings were done, I improvised and added a cup of milk and a dash of cream to Lucy's recipe...like I remembered my mother doing.

When all the cooking was finished, Baby Dear and I shared her first serving of Grandma's chicken and dumplings.

B.D. heartily approved. After she finished eating Grandma's chicken and dumplings, she crawled around on the floor and played with her toys, satisfied and comforted by the warm food.

I was satisfied and comforted as well.

Yes, the dumplings were good.

But most of all I was comforted by using my friend's recipe and my mother's rolling pin.

It was so lovely to remember all the good times shared in those kitchens. And it was lovely to share a good time in my kitchen with my own little granddaughter.

That's what comfort food really does…it nourishes your heart and soul. And my heart and soul are very full.

Chapter 2:
Entrees and Meat Dishes

"I don't like food that's too carefully arranged; it makes me think that the chef is spending too much time arranging and not enough time cooking. If I wanted a picture I'd buy a painting."

~ Andy Rooney

I am unsuccessful at making meat loaf. I'm not sure what I do wrong, but the loaf resembles a lumpy brick and the sauce sticks to the top of it without adding much flavor to the concoction. After years of trying to make a good meat loaf, I finally gave up and started making a de-constructed version of the ingredients that I call meat lump. It's tasty, satisfying, and inexpensive.

MEAT LUMP

1 lb. lean ground beef

1 pkg. dry onion soup (the soup is quite salty, so no extra salt is necessary)

1 egg

¼ to ½ cup whole oatmeal

1 large (28 oz.) can crushed tomatoes

- Place ground beef, onion soup mix, beaten egg, and oatmeal in a bowl or baking pan. Using hands, combine all ingredients until well mixed.
- Pat beef mixture in to patties and place in cookware. You can cook meat lump in a skillet on the range top, or you can bake it.

*If cooking in a skillet, brown the patties lightly on each side. Add crushed tomatoes. Bring to boil.

- Cover and let simmer at low heat for 20 minutes or until meat is thoroughly cooked through and tomatoes have made a sauce.

*If baking, place the patties in a small baking pan, sides touching. Pour crushed tomatoes over them. Cover with lid or foil.

- Bake at 350 degrees for 30 minutes.
- Uncover and continue baking for another 10 minutes to brown.

Serve with your choice of steamed rice, mashed potatoes, or simple macaroni and cheese.

COLOSSAL CHEESEBURGER

1 ½ lb. ground beef

½ cup chopped onion

½ tsp. salt

¼ tsp. pepper

½ to 1 tsp. chili powder

8 oz. can tomato sauce

2 (8 oz.) cans refrigerated crescent dinner rolls

1 c. shredded cheddar cheese

1 Tbsp. milk

Sesame seeds (optional, but they add nicely to the flavor)

- Preheat oven to 375 degrees. Grease 12 inch pizza pan.
- In a large frying pan, brown ground meat and onions. Stir in salt, pepper, chili powder, and tomato sauce.
- Separate crescent into 16 triangles. Arrange 13 triangles around the prepared pan, in a spoke fashion with the narrow tips of triangles extending over pan edge about 5 inches. Press 3 remaining triangles in center of pan to cover. Seal perforations.
- Spread meat mixture over dough, sprinkle with cheese.
- Bring dough up over filling to the center; pinch edges to seal.
- Brush dough with milk; sprinkle with sesame seeds.
- Bake at 375 degrees for 20 to 25 minutes until golden brown and crust is no longer doughy.
- Makes 5 to 6 serving

MEATBALL & POTATO SUPPER

1 lb. ground beef

2/3 cup fine, dry bread crumbs (or ½ cup oatmeal)

2/3 cup evaporated milk

1 tsp. salt

½ c. finely chopped onion (or ¼ cup dehydrated onions)

2 Tbsp. flour

2 Tbsp. hot cooking oil

½ cup sliced onion

3 cups thinly sliced, peeled, uncooked potatoes

1 tsp. salt

¼ tsp. ground black pepper

1 cup very hot water

- In a bowl, mix the beef, bread crumbs, milk, salt and finely chopped onion.
- Wet hands to keep meat mixture from sticking to them, then shape meat in to 12 balls.
- Roll meatballs, one at a time, in flour.
- Brown meatballs on all sides in hot fat in skillet.
- Cook onions slowly for 5 minutes.
- Put potatoes on top of meatballs and sliced onions.
- Sprinkle salt and pepper over potatoes.
- Pour hot water over potatoes.
- Cover tightly and cook over low heat until potatoes (or about 20 minutes.)
- Serve hot.

MEXICAN CASSEROLE

1 ½ lbs. ground beef

1 large onion, chopped

1 can cram of mushroom soup

1 can cream of chicken soup

2 small cans chopped green chilies

2 small cans taco sauce

1 cup grated Velveeta cheese

1 large package tortilla chips (I prefer Doritos brand)

- Line 9 x 13 casserole dish with slightly crushed tortilla chips.
- Cook ground beef and onions together in skillet on stove top until done, but not browned.
- Add all other ingredients to skillet, except cheese. Mix together and heat.
- Pour warm mixture in tortilla chip lined dish you have already prepared.
- Top with grated cheese.
- Bake at 400 degrees until cheese melts.

Serve with green salad and pico de gallo or salsa.

ONE DISH MEAL

1 lb. ground beef

1/3 cup chopped onion

1/3 cup chopped bell pepper

1 tsp. Worcestershire sauce

2 tsp. chili powder

¾ tsp. salt

1 can tomatoes

1 can whole kernel corn

1 pkg cornbread mix, mixed according to directions (the individual size that makes only one pan of cornbread)

- Combine ground beef, onion, bell pepper, and salt in skillet.
- Cook over medium heat until brown.
- Mix remaining ingredients and let simmer 10 minutes.
- Top with prepared, uncooked cornbread mixture and bake 25 to 30 minutes at 425 degrees or until nicely browned.

BEEFY MEXICAN CORNBREAD

This is a spicy, tasty meal in a skillet. Just add a salad and you have a full meal.

½ lb. ground beef

2-3 Tbsp vegetable oil

1 cup self-rising cornmeal

1 cup buttermilk

1 (14.75 oz) can cream style corn

2 eggs (beaten)

1 large sweet yellow onion

1 small can (4 oz) of chopped jalapenos or green chilies (these are optional)

1 cup shredded cheddar cheese.

- Put oil in a 10 cast-iron skillet or 9 x 13 pan. Place in 350 degree oven to pre-heat.
- Brown ground beef, drain fat.
- Mix cornmeal, buttermilk, cream style corn, and beaten eggs in a large bowl until well mixed.
- When skillet or pan is hot, pour half of the batter in it.
- Spread beef, onion, and peppers (If using chilies or jalapenos) over the batter. Then sprinkle with cheese.
- Top with the other half of the batter.
- Bake for 45 to 50 minutes or until golden brown.
- Allow to cool slightly before cutting or flipping on to serving plate.

OVEN-BAKED FRITO PIE

1 lb. lean ground beef

1 can (16 oz) chili beans

1 can (8 oz) tomato sauce

1 can (15 oz) diced tomatoes

1 cup shredded cheddar cheese

3 ½ cups Fritos (corn chips)

1 ¼ cup sour cream

- Cook ground beef until light browned, drain fat.
- Stir in beans, tomato sauce, diced tomatoes and ¼ cup of cheese to make a chili sauce. You can also add a packet of low sodium taco seasoning if you want it spicier.
- Sprinkle 1 cup of chips in bottom of lightly greased 8x8 baking dish.
- Cover with chili sauce. Bake at 350 degrees for 20 minutes.
- Remove from oven. Spread sour cream over chili and top with remaining chips and cheese.
- Bake for 4 to 5 minutes longer to melt cheese.

Serve hot. Add greens or salad to complete your meal.

If God had intended us to follow recipes, He wouldn't have given us Grandmothers. – Linda Henley –

When I decided to write this book, I asked my cousins and friends if they would like to add any of their favorite recipes from their grandmothers. Every single one of them said, "She didn't use recipes. I don't have any of her recipes written down."

The other thing that every single one of my cousins said was, "She made the very best fried chicken. I wish I knew how to fry chicken like my Grandma/Nanny/Memaw/Granny."

When I was a 19 year old newlywed, I was armed with a good cast iron skillet, a sharp knife, and the confidence that I could cut up and fry a chicken. I had watched my mother do it a thousand times. And, pardon my bragging, but I was pretty good at it. Of course my platters of fried chicken didn't quite measure up to Mama's or any of my aunts', but then…whose could have?

The following recipe is as close as I can come to the fried chicken prepared by Grandma/Nanny/Memaw/Granny.

PAN-FRIED CHICKEN

1 ½ cups all-purpose flour

1 ½ tsp. salt

½ tsp. pepper

1 broiler/fryer chicken (3 to 4 lbs.), cut up

Oil or shortening for frying

- Wash and cut up the chicken and remove skin.
- Pat chicken pieces dry with a paper towel.
- Mix flour, salt, and pepper together.
- Put in small paper bag or a plastic bag (zipper closed bags work well).
- Place a few pieces of chicken at a time in the bag. Shake to coat.
- Heat ½ inch of oil or shortening in a large skillet over medium heat.
- Place chicken in skillet and fry until browned on all sides.
- Reduce heat; cover and cook for 30-35 minutes or until juices run clear. Turn occasionally.
- Uncover and cook 5 minutes longer to make crisp.
- Drain on paper towels.

*Note: I always remove the skin from chicken before cooking. I don't like chicken skin.

OVEN FRIED CHICKEN

3 lb. frying chicken, cut up

1 cup. Buttermilk

¾ c. flour

½ tsp. paprika

1 Tbsp. instant minced onions

1 tsp. salt

½ tsp. ground black pepper

½ tsp. thyme

½ c. melted butter

- Cover chicken pieces with buttermilk; set aside in refrigerator for 1 hour.
- Combine rest of ingredients except butter.
- Roll chicken pieces in flour mixture.
- Melt butter in a shallow baking pan in oven.
- Place chicken in pan, turn to coat with melted butter.
- Arrange in single layer (skin side down if you leave the skin on).
- Bake at 350 degrees for ½ hour, turn chicken and bake another ½ hour or until browned and tender.

Use the pan drippings with flour and milk to make gravy.

CRUSTY PARMESAN OVEN FRIED CHICKEN

1 cup bread crumbs

¼ cup grated Parmesan cheese

1 tsp. salt

¼ tsp. garlic powder

¼ tsp. pepper

1 TBSP chopped parsley (if desired)

1 (2 ½ to 3 lb.) chicken, cut up

½ cup melted margarine or butter (can use olive oil or cooking oil if desired)

- Combine bread crumbs, cheese, salt, garlic powder and pepper. Add parsley if desired.
- Rinse chicken and pat dry.
- Dip chicken pieces in melted butter and roll in bread crumb mixture.
- Place chicken skin side up (if you choose not to remove the skin) in a large baking dish.
- Bake in 350 degree oven for 1 hour, until tender.

OVEN BARBECUED CHICKEN

1 large fryer, cut up (or use whatever pieces your family likes)

Sauce:

3 Tbsp catsup

2 Tbsp vinegar

2 Tbsp Worcestershire sauce

4 Tbsp water

3 Tbsp oil

3 Tbsp brown sugar

1 tsp. salt

1 tsp. mustard

1 tsp. paprika

½ tsp. chili powder

- Season chicken lightly with salt and pepper. Place in ungreased baking pan.
- Pour sauce over chicken and bake uncovered for 2 hours at 300 degrees, basting often.

CHEESY CHICKEN CASSEROLE

3 cups cooked chicken, chopped

2 cans (10.75 oz each) cream of chicken soup

2 cups shredded Cheddar cheese

3 cups Progresso™ panko crispy bread crumbs or any dry stuffing mix

6 tablespoons butter or margarine, melted

- Heat oven to 350°F.
- Place chicken in bottom of ungreased 13 x 9-inch baking dish.
- Spoon soup evenly over chicken and top with shredded cheese.
- In medium bowl stir together melted butter and breadcrumbs.
- Sprinkle over baking dish. Bake 35 to 40 minutes or until bubbly.

CHICKEN POT PIE

1/3 cup butter

1/3 cup all-purpose flour

1/3 cup chopped onion

½ tsp salt

¼ tsp pepper

1 ¾ cups chicken broth

2/3 cup milk

2 ½ to 3 cups cut-up cooked chicken or turkey

1 box (10 oz) frozen peas and carrots*

1 package (15 oz) refrigerated pie crusts, softened as directed on box

*Use a deep pie pan or a 9x13 casserole dish to bake this. You want the bottom crust to line the sides of the pan, so if you use a 9x13 pan, you will need to roll your bottom pie crust into a 13 inch square. Your top crust will need to be rolled into an 11 inch square.

If using a round deep dish pie pan, you can roll or stretch the pre-prepared crust to cover the side of the dish to the rim.

To prepare chicken mixture:

- In medium sized saucepan, melt butter over medium heat.
- Stir in flour, onion, salt and pepper.
- Cook, stirring constantly, until mixture is bubbly; remove from heat.
- Stir in broth and milk. Heat to boiling, stirring constantly. Boil and stir 1 minute.
- Stir in chicken and peas and carrots; remove from heat.

To prepare Crust:

- Roll 1 pie crust into 13-inch square or, if using a deep pie pan, stretch crust to cover the bottom and sides to rim of pan. Ease crust into ungreased baking dish.
- Pour chicken mixture into crust-lined dish.
- Roll remaining pie crust into 11-inch square.
- Place square over chicken mixture.
- Turn edges of pie crust under; flute edge.

Bake at 425 degrees about 35 minutes or until golden brown.

SMOTHERED CHICKEN CASSEROLE

1 Tbsp oil

4 boneless skinless chicken thighs

½ tsp garlic salt

¼ tsp pepper

6 oz uncooked angel hair pasta

1 can (10 3/4 oz) condensed cream of chicken soup

1 ¼ cups half-and-half

½ tsp smoked paprika

2 cups frozen broccoli florets, cut into smaller pieces

3 slices crispy, cooked bacon, crumbled

- Heat oven to 350°F.
- Heat oil over medium heat in a large skillet.
- Add chicken thighs to skillet. Sprinkle with garlic salt and pepper.
- Cook chicken 8 to 10 minutes, turning once, until golden brown and juice of chicken is clear when thickest part is cut (at least 165°F).
- Cook pasta as directed on package; drain.

- In large bowl, mix soup, half-and-half and paprika; reserve 3/4 cup sauce.
- Stir in cooked pasta and frozen broccoli.
- Spray large casserole dish with cooking spray.
- Place pasta mixture in casserole; top with chicken thighs.
- Spoon reserved sauce over chicken thighs.
- Top with bacon.
- Cover and bake 20 minutes, then uncover and bake 10 to 15 minutes or until sauce bubbles.

GRANDMA'S CHICKEN AND DUMPLINGS

You can buy a whole chicken that's intact, a chicken that's already cut up, or single packages of chicken breasts and thighs. This recipe was written long before those options were commonly available at grocery stores.

1 – 3 to 4 lb. stewing hen or large broiler-fryer

3 cups sifted all-purpose flour

1 tsp. salt

2 tsp. baking powder

½ cup shortening (I used Crisco)

1 cup milk

- Cut chicken into serving pieces and place in large kettle with salted water to cover.
- Cover kettle with lid.
- Bring to boil, then reduce flame to simmer and cook until chicken is tender.
- While chicken is cooking combine flour, salt, baking powder.
- With fork or two knives, cut in shortening. Add milk and mix well.
- Turn out onto lightly floured board or pastry cloth and knead lightly.
- Roll out to 1/8 inch thickness. Cut into strips.
- When chicken is tender, drop strips into kettle.
- Cover and continue simmering 20 minutes.
- Add milk and cream and allow to heat. Remove from heat and serve.
- Makes 8 hearty servings.

Experienced cooks embellish basic foodstuffs by instinct, intuition, and taste. My mother, aunts, and grandmothers cooked that way: instinctively and intuitively adjusting dishes by taste and by the ingredients that were available. I loved their food. But, oh how I wish they had written down the recipes they developed.

The following recipe is my mother's recipe for turkey and cornbread dressing as dictated to and noted by my sister. It is very, very basic. I don't have enough intuition or instinct to even attempt it.

Turkey & Dressing

Cook 10-12 pound turkey for 2 hours, drain broth.

Dressing

1 pan cornbread

1 lb. loaf of bread

3 eggs beaten

½ cup chopped onions

Poultry seasoning

1 pint chicken broth

Crumble cornbread and dried bread in large bowl.
Add eggs, onions, broth, and poultry seasoning.
Spoon dressing around turkey in large pan.

Stuff dressing in cavity of turkey, continue to cook at 325 degrees for 1 ½ to 2 more hours.

Sounds simple enough, doesn't it?! I'm incapable of reproducing her results. So it's fortunate that I found a recipe that works for me.

CHICKEN AND DRESSING SKILLET BAKE

2 Tbsp butter or margarine

1 cup chopped onions

1 cup chopped celery

1 Tbsp oil

3 cups cubed cooked chicken

1 cup frozen corn

2 (6 oz) packages of cornbread mix like Corn-Kits or Martha White cornbread mix. DO NOT use a sweet cornbread mix.

1 ½ tsp poultry seasoning

1 ¾ cups milk

2 eggs, beaten

- Heat oven to 400 degrees.
- Melt butter in a 10-inch cast iron skillet, over medium heat. Add onions and celery; cook 8 to 10 minutes or until tender, stirring occasionally.
- Spoon onions and celery into large bowl.
- Add oil to same skillet; place in oven and heat for 5 minutes.
- Add all remaining ingredients to onions and celery in bowl; blend well.
- Pour batter over oil in hot skillet.
- Bake at 400 degrees for 29-35 minutes or until golden brown.
- Cut into wedges; serve with chicken gravy if you like.

NOTES:

HAM AND SWEET POTATO CASSEROLE

1 ½ lbs. cooked ham (pre-sliced or slice yourself)

3 lbs. sweet potatoes, cooked

½ cup chopped pecans

1 (8 oz) can sliced pineapple, drained

¾ cup Mrs. Butterworth's syrup

- Bake sweet potatoes, then peel and slice. Or use canned sweet potatoes.
- Arrange alternate slices of potatoes and ham in 9 inch pie pan or in shallow casserole pan.
- Cut pineapple slices in halves; tuck in to casserole.
- Sprinkle nuts over surface.
- Bake in preheated 350 degree oven for 15 minutes.
- Remove from oven and pour syrup over ham, potatoes, pineapple, and pecans.
- Return to oven and bake 15 – 20 more minutes until hot and bubbly.

Makes 6 servings.

PORK CHOPS WITH APPLES

6 pork chops

3 to 4 unpeeled apples, cored and sliced

¼ cup packed brown sugar

½ tsp. cinnamon

- Place pork chops in skillet and brown on all sides, adding salt and pepper to taste.
- Place sliced apples in a buttered baking dish.
- Sprinkle brown sugar and cinnamon over apples.
- Top the apples with chops.
- Cover with casserole lid or foil; then bake at 400 degrees F for 1 hour.

Serves 6.

PORK CHOPS IN MUSHROOM GRAVY

1 Tbsp butter

1 clove garlic, pressed

6 pork chops

salt and pepper to taste

1 (8 ounce) can mushrooms, drained

1 cup dry sherry

1 (10.5 ounce) can beef broth

2 tablespoons cornstarch

2 tablespoons water

Preheat the oven to 350 degrees.

- Melt the butter in a large skillet over medium heat.
- Add garlic, and saute.
- Season pork chops with salt and pepper, then fry them in the skillet just until browned on both sides, about 3 minutes per side.
- Remove the pork chops to a baking pan or Dutch oven. Pour the mushrooms into the skillet with the pork drippings and garlic, and stir in the sherry and beef broth, scraping any bits of pork that are stuck to the pan.
- Bring to a boil, then pour over the pork chops in the baking pan. Cover with a lid, or aluminum foil.

- Bake covered for 45 minutes at 350 degrees, then remove the lid or foil, and continue to bake for another 15 minutes.
- Remove the chops from the pan to a serving platter, and pour juices into skillet.
- Stir together the cornstarch and water.
- Bring juices to a boil.
- Slowly add the cornstarch mixture to the juices, stirring constantly. Lower heat and cook until thickened, about 2 minutes.
- Spoon sauce over the chops, and serve.

NOTES:

Good food is very often, even most often, simple food. – Anthony Bourdain

---

Long before we folks on the Texas plains were introduced to grilled salmon steaks, we ate canned salmon…bones and all. No salmon run the muddy rivers of Texas.

The salmon served at my family's table was formed into patties made from canned salmon mixed with eggs, saltines, and rolled in cornmeal. Then they were fried in lard or Crisco shortening… as God intended.

It was a staple of my childhood. Salmon patties weren't a fancy gourmet meal, but they were a treat we all looked forward to. We had simple tastes.

This recipe is my version of my Mama's style of salmon patties. It comes close to being as good as hers were…close, but not quite.

SALMON PATTIES

1 - 12 oz. can of Pink Salmon

Crushed saltine crackers (about ½ cup, add more or less to adjust moisture)

1 or 2 whole eggs

½ cup corn meal (or you can use corn meal mix if you have it)

½ cup cooking oil

*You can add chopped green onions, chopped bell peppers, chopped onions, or herbs to your liking. I prefer this very plain version.

*Note: *Canned salmon contains fish skin and bones and is canned in a liquid. You can remove the bones and skin and drain the liquid if you like. I don't, but this is a personal preference. The skin and bones do not bother me; I mash them well and mix up with the meat. I think the liquid makes the croquettes more moist once cooked.*

Put corn meal in a plate or pie pan. Set aside.

- Open canned salmon and empty into a bowl. Mix contents with a spoon, crushing bones if you leave them.
- Crush saltine crackers with a rolling pin. They should be very fine. This helps bind your mixture together. Sprinkle in to bowl.
- Add egg or eggs to salmon and crackers.
- Mix together, making a mixture that can be made into a clump or ball. This will be very moist, but should hold together. Do not mix too thoroughly because it will become a gooey, squishy mess.
- Roll salmon mixture lightly in corn meal.
- Place in hot oil in skillet. Cook until browned; flip to other side and brown.
- Remove from skillet and drain on paper towel.

FANCIER SALMON CROQUETTE

1 - 12 oz can of Pink Salmon

2 whole eggs

¼ cup chopped Onions

¼ cup chopped Bell Pepper

2 Tbsp. yellow corn meal

½ tsp. salt

½ tsp. garlic powder

2 Tbsp. mayonnaise

1 tsp. Worcestershire sauce

1 tsp. hot sauce

½ tsp ground black pepper

1 slice crumbled white bread

¼ cup flour

- Open canned salmon and drain. Remove bones and skin.
- Place salmon in large bowl, flake with a fork.
- Add two whole eggs, chopped onions, and chopped bell peppers.
- Add corn meal, salt, garlic powder, mayonnaise, Worcestershire sauce, hot sauce, and ground pepper.
- Crumble the bread and place in bowl.
- Gently mix all ingredients together, but do not over work the mix.
- If the mixture is too moist, add flour as needed to adjust the consistency.
- Divide and shape the mixture into four patties. Set aside.
- Heat the skillet to medium heat and add oil or shortening to fry.
- Place patties in oil, brown the bottom, then turn to brown the other side.
- When both sides are brown, remove from skillet and place on a paper towel to drain.

Chapter 3: Eggs

I have to confess that I have burned boiled eggs before and even unwittingly created small bombs in a saucepan by boiling the eggs dry and exploding them. I had to learn how to boil eggs successfully.

There is an art to it…or at least instructions on how to do it.

HOW TO BOIL AN EGG

- Place eggs in a single layer in a saucepan large enough to hold them.
- Cover eggs by 1 inch with cold water.
- Heat water over high heat just to boiling.
- Remove from burner.

- Cover pan.
- Let eggs stand in hot water about 12 to 15 minutes.
- Drain immediately and serve warm.
- Or cool completely under cold running water or in bowl of ice water, then refrigerate in a tightly covered container.

.

I argued with my cousin about this method. But, since she prepares perfect eggs this way and NEVER creates exploding egg bombs, I have to concede that she is right and I am wrong.

There it is… in print… calf rope.

Love and eggs are best when they are fresh. – Russian Proverb

---

How to tell if a raw egg is fresh: place egg in a pan of cold water. If it stands on end, it is not very fresh and should be tossed or used immediately. If it settles down on its side, it is fresh.

*If boiled eggs are shelled, you can refrigerate them but should use them within 1 day. If left unshelled, eggs can be stored for up to 5 days before using

STUFFED or DEVILED EGGS

Wicked chickens lay deviled eggs. – Anonymous

---

6 shelled, hard cooked eggs

¼ cup mayonnaise

Pinch of ground black or white pepper

¼ tsp. salt

¼ tsp. prepared mustard

1 tsp. minced green onions

1Tbsp. pickle juice or 1 Tbsp. pickle relish (you can use sweet or dill pickle relish, whatever suits your taste)

Bacon bits (optional)

- Cut eggs in halves. Remove yolks and set aside in bowl.
- Mash yolks and add remaining ingredients. Mix well until smooth.
- Generously refill whites, rounding each half.
- Sprinkle tops with crispy bacon bits, if using.

FANCY DEVILED EGGS

12 hard boiled eggs.

2 tsp. prepared mustard

1 ½ tsp. Worcestershire sauce

1/4 tsp. pepper

3 TBSP mayonnaise

2 TBSP lemon juice

¼ tsp. salt

Paprika

- Cut eggs in half.
- Remove yolks, combine with remaining ingredients, blending well.
- Refill egg whites.
- Garnish by sprinkling lightly with paprika.

CHUNKY EGG SALAD

6 hard cooked eggs

½ cup celery

1 TBSP minced green pepper

1 tsp. minced onion

¼ cup mayonnaise

½ tsp. Worcestershire sauce

Dash of liquid pepper

1 TBSP vinegar

1 tsp. salt

1/8 tsp. ground pepper

Crisp greens

- Wash greens and set aside to dry.
- Slice eggs or cut in pieces and put in mixing bowl.
- Add other ingredients, except greens.
- Mix together.
- Refrigerate the egg mixture.
- Serve on crisp greens to make a beautiful egg salad.

People who love to eat are always the best people. – Julia Child

---

Every weekend I call my best friend and we talk for an hour or three. We've been best friends for over 50 years now so we have a lot to talk about.

Do we talk about politics, religion, and sex?

Nope.

Do we gossip about other friends or complain about our work? Or gripe about the high price of …oh, whatever has a high price that week?

Nope.

We only discuss the truly important things of life. We talk about what we ate and what we read during the previous week.

We both love to eat…and cook for our families…and we both love to read, so that's what we talk about. We share opinions and reviews about what we read. We discuss the authors; we suggest books for each other to read.

Then we describe what we ate and share the recipes. The next best thing to eating good food is talking about eating good food.

When we were little girls, we used to lie side-by-side…on either of our beds or on the floor…or sit in a chair together…and read the same book together. We waited until the other finished until we turned the page. When we got older, we read magazines the same way…side-by-side…happy to share the words.

Sometimes we would read recipes from magazines and convince my mother to let us try them out in her kitchen. I remember one spectacular mess we made that had dumplings and potatoes cooked together. It was awful and even my patient, put-upon mother was disgusted.

So now that we're older… (even trending toward OLD)…we still share our reading and cooking adventures. We just do it by phone now. But if we had the opportunity to flop across the bed, we'd still read books together, side-by-side, waiting until the other finished before turning the page.

We would look at cookbooks and try out new recipes.

Sunday Brunch Eggs is one of the recipes we've shared in recent years. My friend found it and told me about it and I had to try it myself. It was delightfully delicious! And although it is a bit more expensive than the frugal pantry I try to live from, I think you will like it, too.

SUNDAY BRUNCH EGGS (Or Sunday Supper)

12 slices Canadian bacon

12 slices swiss cheese

12 eggs

1 cup whipping cream

1/3 cup grated parmesan cheese

12 slices toast (optional)

- Place Canadian bacon in greased 13 x 9 inch baking dish; top with Swiss cheese.
- Break an egg over each piece of cheese.
- Pour cream over eggs; sprinkle Parmesan cheese.
- Bake at 375 degrees for 20-25 minutes or until eggs reach desired stage of doneness.
- Remove from oven and let stand for 5 minutes.
- Cut between each egg to serve.

Serve on toast or ½ toasted English muffin if desired.

*Fruit salad or sliced fruit is a good companion for this dish.

Chapter 4: Soups & Stews

"Only the pure in heart can make a good soup." - Ludwig van Beethoven -

---

Most mothers and grandmothers have a specialty soup to soothe an upset tummy or fight a savage head cold. Some mothers use chicken soup. Others suggest hot and sour soup to open the stuffy nasal passages.

My mother made potato soup to make us feel better when we were sick or even just a little sad. It was a simple soup made with boiled potatoes, butter, salt and pepper, and milk and served with saltine crackers.

One of my early memories is of lying in my parents' bed while suffering from a sore throat and being served a bowl of potato soup with crackers. I remember thinking how special that was to be served soup in bed like Loretta Young.

I still smile when I think of it. I was the indulged baby of the family and might have been just a bit spoiled, but the truth was that she made her potato soup for anyone who felt under the weather.

I'm pretty sure Mama's potato soup had magical healing powers. Perhaps it was the love that she stirred into it that did it.

MAGIC POTATO SOUP

3 to 4 medium potatoes (I usually use Russet, but you can use whatever you prefer)

¼ to ½ tsp. salt (to taste)

Pinch of ground black pepper

8 cups water

2 cups whole milk

2 TBSP butter

- Peel potatoes and cut into chunks. (If using new red potatoes, you can scrub and leave peels on.)
- Place in saucepan with at least 8 cups water.
- Bring to boil, then lower heat to medium, cooking potatoes until soft.
- Drain water, leaving about ¼ cup water in pan.
- Mash potatoes slightly, leaving some chunks.
- Add salt and pepper to taste.
- Add butter and stir in milk.

Heat, stirring constantly, until milk is hot and the butter, salt and pepper have blended with milk and potato combination.

CHEESY POTATO SOUP

1 to 3 large baking potatoes

½ cup chopped onions

½ cup sliced carrots

½ cup sliced celery

1 14.5 oz can chicken broth

1 tsp. salt

½ tsp. pepper

1 cup Velveeta or American cheese, cubed

1 cup milk

- Peel and cube potatoes into large soup pot. Add onion, carrots, celery, broth, 1 broth can of water, and seasonings.
- Bring to boil. Reduce heat to low and cook for 15 minutes or until vegetables are tender.
- Mash vegetables to desired texture. (I like mine chunky because I prefer to have a nice soupy base to crumble cornbread in).
- Add cheese and milk. Stir while cheese melts and milk heats through. Serve with crackers, cornbread, or bread of your choice.

WHITE CHICKEN CHILI

1 Tbsp vegetable oil

4 skinless, boneless chicken breast halves, cubed

4 tsp. chili powder

2 tsp. ground cumin

1 large onion, chopped

1 medium green pepper, chopped

1 can chicken broth

¾ cup water

1 ½ cups frozen whole kernel corn

2 cans cannellini beans (white kidney)

2 TBSP shredded Cheddar cheese

- Heat oil in large saucepan on medium high heat.
- Add chicken, chili powder, cumin, onion and pepper. Cook until chicken is cooked through and vegetables are tender, stirring often.
- Stir broth, water, corn and beans in saucepan. Heat to a boil. Reduce heat to low. Cover and cook 5 minutes, stirring occasionally.
- Serve and sprinkle with cheese.

MEXICAN CHICKEN CHOWDER

4 chicken breasts, cooked and cubed

½ cup each chopped onion and bell pepper

1 tsp vegetable oil

1 (10 oz) diced tomatoes & green chilies (Rotel is a familiar brand)

1 (32 oz) package frozen hashbrown potatoes (cubes not grated)

½ tsp each salt, garlic salt and black pepper

2 cups Velveeta or American cheese, cubed

2 (10.75 oz) cans Cream of Chicken soup

- In large Dutch oven, sauté onion and bell pepper in oil.
- Stir in tomatoes with green chilies, hashbrowns, and seasonings.
- Add 4 cups of water and simmer over medium heat for about 45 minutes or until potatoes are tender.
- Cube cheese and add to mixture.
- Cook and stir until cheese is melted.
- Add chicken and chicken soup.
- Heat thoroughly and serve.

MY FAVORITE TOMATO SOUP

1 - 28 oz. can Italian style stewed tomatoes

16 oz. chicken broth

¼ cup chopped or sliced onions

10 ¾ oz. can condensed tomato soup

1 soup can of whole milk (1 ¼ cup)

½ soup can of heavy cream (3/4 cup)

Fresh grated Parmesan cheese

- Place stewed tomatoes, onion, and chicken broth in large pot and bring to boil. Lower heat and simmer for 15 minutes.
- Let cool 20 minutes. Place in blender and blend on high until liquefied.
- Put back in large pot and add condensed tomato soup, stirring until well-blended. Add milk and cream.
- Re-heat on low temperature, stirring often to keep from scorching.
- When warm, serve in soup bowls and top with Parmesan cheese.

Serve with warm, crusty French bread and green salad.

HAMBURGER SOUP

½ lb to 1 lb ground beef

½ cup chopped onions

1 can chicken broth

1 broth can of water

1 large baking potato or 3 small potatoes (depending on your personal preference for potatoes)

1 12- 16 oz. pkg. frozen mixed vegetables

1 large can crushed tomatoes

½ tsp. salt

¼ tsp. ground black pepper

- Cook ground beef and onions over low heat until onions are clear and beef is no longer red. Do not overcook.
- Drain on paper towel; then place in large pot.
- Add broth and water.
- Peel and cut potato in small chunks; add to pot.
- Bring to boil; cover pot; lower heat and simmer until potatoes are tender.
- Add frozen vegetables, salt, and pepper. Simmer 10 minutes.
- Add crushed tomatoes and simmer another 10 minutes. Serve with hot cornbread.

PASTA FAGIOLI

1 cup shell macaroni

2 tablespoons olive oil, divided

1 pound spicy Italian sausage, casing removed

3 cloves garlic, minced

1 onion, diced

3 carrots, peeled and diced

2 stalks celery, diced

3 cups chicken broth

1 (16-ounce) can tomato sauce

1 (15-ounce) can diced tomatoes

1 teaspoon dried basil

1 teaspoon dried oregano

3/4 teaspoon dried thyme

Salt and freshly ground black pepper, to taste

1 (15-ounce) can red kidney beans, drained and rinsed

1 (15-ounce) can great northern beans, drained and rinsed

- In a large pot of boiling salted water, cook pasta according to package instructions; drain well and set aside.
- Heat 1 Tbsp olive oil in a large stockpot or Dutch oven over medium heat.
- Add Italian sausage to the skillet and cook until browned, about 3-5 minutes, making sure to crumble the sausage as it cooks.
- Drain excess fat and set aside.
- Add remaining 1Tbsp oil to the stockpot.
- Stir in garlic, onion, carrots and celery.
- Cook, stirring occasionally, until tender, about 3-4 minutes.
- Whisk in chicken broth, tomato sauce, diced tomatoes, basil, oregano, thyme, Italian sausage and 1 cup water; season with salt and pepper, to taste.
- Bring to a boil; reduce heat and simmer, covered, until vegetables are tender, about 10-15 minutes.
- Stir in pasta and beans until heated through.
- Serve immediately.

UNSTUFFED CABBAGE SOUP

1 medium cabbage, chopped

1 lb. lean ground beef or 1 lb. pork sausage or 1 lb. Italian sausage

1 cup yellow onion, chopped

2 garlic cloves, minced (more if you like)

1 28 oz. can stewed tomatoes or crushed tomatoes

8 ounces chicken broth or 8 ounces vegetarian chicken broth

1/4 teaspoon cayenne (more if you like) (optional)

1 tablespoon Worcestershire sauce

1/2 teaspoon nutmeg (optional)

salt and pepper, to taste

1/2 cup rice, raw

- Saute onion and garlic in a large skillet for about a minute.
- Add meat and cook, stirring often, until meat is no longer pink.
- Drain well and return to pan.
- Add broth.
- Meanwhile, remove tough outer leaves from cabbage & remove core. Chop cabbage. (shredded and bagged cabbage or coleslaw mix works great and saves this step)
- Add cabbage to pan and simmer with the meat just until the cabbage begins to soften.
- Add remaining ingredients and bring to a boil.
- Reduce heat and allow to simmer until rice is done or place in a crock pot and cook on low for 2 hours or until done.

NAVY BEAN SOUP

1 ½ cups Great Northern beans

1 quart water

1 ham bone

1 clove garlic, minced (or already prepared minced garlic)

1 white or yellow onion, diced

½ cup celery, diced

1 medium diced potato

½ tsp dried thyme, crushed

½ tsp salt

¼ tsp pepper

- ***Pre-soak beans: In a Dutch oven or large stock pot, bring water and beans to boil. Turn off burner. Cover and let stand 1 hour.***

- Drain soaked beans, reserving all liquid. Measure this liquid and add enough water to make 2 quarts exactly.
- Place beans, water and ham bone in pot. Cover and simmer for 2 hours.
- Add potatoes, onion, celery, garlic, thyme, salt and pepper.
- Simmer for 1 more hour.
- Take 1 cup of beans with liquid and puree in blender.
- Add pureed beans back to soup to thicken.
- Remove ham bone and strip meat. Return meat to pot; discard bone.
- Adjust seasonings to taste, adding more if necessary.

Makes 8 to 10 servings.

Chapter 5: Vegetables & Salads

"It's difficult to think anything but pleasant thoughts while eating a homegrown tomato."
- Lewis Grizzard -

Last spring I planted a vegetable garden. I planted potatoes and plugged in some onions in the soft dirt on top of them. Even though we were in the third year of drought and record setting warm temperatures and it hadn't rained since I don't know when…I planted it anyway.

All I can say is that hope springs eternal in a gardener's heart.

In the days after I planted, I dug up more patches of dirt. I pulled out the Bermuda grass sprigs, emptied some bags of cow manure onto the dirt clods and worked the manure in with a shovel. I threw in some leaf mold and compost.

Then I hoped for the best and prayed for rain.

I grew up on a farm. And every year my mother planted a garden. She didn't let dry weather stop her. Every year, she harvested a bountiful crop of potatoes, corn, squash, green beans, pinto beans, black-eyed peas, English peas, radishes, onions, okra, spinach, cabbage, lettuce, cucumbers, dill, beets, and tomatoes. What we didn't eat fresh each day, she put away for later.

My mother canned the produce in glass Mason jars, carefully cleaning and storing the jars after we emptied each one at mealtime during the year.

She blanched corn, peas, and squash and froze them. She pickled beets and cucumbers and made sweet bread-and-butter pickles and salty dills. She made chow-chow with the end-of-season green tomatoes.

We ate like kings almost the whole year round thanks to Mama's diligence and hard work. And it wasn't just my family that ate like that…all my relatives ate well too, because all my aunts gardened, harvested, and canned their own food.

With a background like this, how can I help but try again and again, year after year, to produce some tomatoes and squash, potatoes and onions, spinach and lettuce right here in my back yard? I'm not the gardener that my mother was, but some years I have a little bit of luck and fresh tomatoes.

Last year I had beautiful tomato vines and I watered them faithfully. They were covered with little yellow blooms, but didn't produce even ONE tomato. After my water bill reached over $100 in June, I began to slack off the watering. I finally gave up and bought my fresh tomatoes at the Farmer's Market.

Gardening is kind of like Life, really. You sow what you hope to reap, till and plant, spread the bull hockey around, and just hope and pray for the best. And the prize is thinking pleasant thoughts while eating homegrown tomatoes.

SQUASH PIE

2 eggs

½ cup grated Parmesan cheese

¼ cup cooking oil

Minced garlic (to taste…it doesn't take much)

Dash salt

Pinch of ground pepper

Dash oregano

1 ½ cups sliced squash (yellow or zucchini or a combination)

½ cup diced onions

½ cup baking mix (I used Bisquick Gluten Free)

- Mix first 7 ingredients, stirring until well blended.
- Stir in squash, onions, and baking mix.
- Lightly grease a 9 inch or smaller pie pan. Bake in preheated 350 degree oven for 25 minutes or until browned on top. Makes 4 small servings.

*The recipe makes a lovely, egg-y, light dish. I used it as an entrée and served it with a leaf lettuce and tomato salad tossed in lemon and olive oil.

To use my granddaughter's description…it was Deeewicious!

SQUASH CASSEROLE

3 medium yellow squash

1 onion, chopped

½ cup fine bread crumbs or cracker crumbs

1/3 cup shredded Cheddar cheese

1 egg, beaten

½ tsp. salt

¼ tsp pepper

4 TBSP margarine or butter, divided

- Cook squash and onion in a small amount of salted water until tender. Drain and set aside.
- Mix bread crumbs (reserving 1 TBSP for top), cheese, egg, salt, pepper, and 2 TBSPs butter/margarine together.
- Spoon into the bottom of a greased casserole dish.
- Put squash and onions on top of bread crumb mixture.
- Top with remaining crumbs; dot with 2 TBSPs margarine/butter.
- Bake at 375 degrees for 10 minutes or until brown.

GARDEN –STUFFED YELLOW SQUASH

6 medium-size yellow squash

1 cup chopped onion

1 cup chopped tomato

1 ½ cup finely chopped green pepper

1 Tbsp chopped fresh basil (or 1 tsp dried)

Dash of pepper

1 cup shredded Cheddar cheese

2 Tbsp butter or margarine

3 slices bacon, cooked crisp and crumbled or 3 Tbsp. bacon bits

- Wash squash. Leave whole.
- Cover with water in stock pot or other large pot. Bring to a boil.
- Cover, reduce heat and simmer 8-9 minutes or until squash is tender but still firm.
- Drain and cool slightly.
- Cut squash in half lengthwise, removed and discard seeds leaving a firm shell.
- Combine onion, tomato, green pepper, basil, salt and pepper in a bowl. Stir in cheese.
- Place squash shells in a 9 x 13 oblong baking dish.
- Spoon vegetable mixture into shells. Dot with butter.
- Sprinkle with bacon.
- Bake uncovered at 400 degrees for 20 minutes.

GREEN CHILI SQUASH

1 lb. yellow squash, thinly sliced (8 cups)

1 medium onion, chopped

2 Tbsp water

16 oz. sour cream

2 cups Monterey Jack cheese, shredded

½ tsp salt

¼ tsp pepper

1 cup crushed cheese-flavored tortilla chips (like Nacho flavored Doritos)

- Combine first 3 ingredients in 11 x 7 inch baking dish sprayed with cooking spray.
- Cover with heavy duty plastic wrap. Fold back one corner so steam can escape.
- Microwave on HIGH 14 to 16 minutes or until squash is almost tender, stirring once.
- Drain well.
- Stir together sour cream, chilies and next 4 ingredients in a large bowl.
- Add squash and mix.
- Place half of mixture in baking dish and sprinkle with half of crushed chips.
- Repeat layers.

Bake at 350 degrees for 20 minutes.

ZUCCHINI PARMESAN CRISPS

½ cup vegetable oil

1 cup Panko*

½ cup grated Parmesan cheese

2 zucchinis, thinly sliced to 1/4-inch thick rounds

½ cup all-purpose flour

2 large eggs, beaten

- Heat vegetable oil in a large skillet over medium high heat.
- In a large bowl, combine Panko and Parmesan; set aside.
- Working in batches, dredge zucchini rounds in flour, dip into eggs, then dredge in Panko mixture, pressing to coat.
- Add zucchini rounds to the skillet, 5 or 6 at a time, and cook until evenly golden and crispy, about 1 minute on each side. Transfer to a paper towel-lined plate.
- Serve immediately.

*Panko is a Japanese-style breadcrumb and can be found in the Asian section of your grocery store.

SOUTHERN LIFE

If you want a glimpse of Southern life,
Come close and walk with me;
I'll tell you all the simple things,
That you are bound to see
You'll see mockingbirds and bumblebees,
Magnolia blossoms and dogwood trees;
Caterpillars on the step,
Wooden porches cleanly swept;
Watermelons on the vine,
Strong majestic Georgia pines
Rocking chairs and front yard swings
Junebugs flying on a string
Turnip greens and hot cornbread,

Coleslaw and barbecue
Fried okra, fried corn, fried green tomatoes,
Fried pies and pickles too.
There's ice cold tea that's syrupy sweet,
And cool, green grass beneath your feet;
Catfish nipping in the lake,
And fresh young boys on the make.
You'll see all these things
And much, much more,
In a way of life, that I adore.

By Patricia Neely-Dorsey

We Southern cooks take a lot of criticism because we fry our vegetables. We fry okra and summer squash and zucchini squash. We fry green tomatoes and left-over mashed potatoes and fresh cabbage and corn cut from the cob.

No matter how much criticism we receive for our cooking methods, we just keep on frying our vegetables. We have compromised by changing our grease from lard to vegetable oil, but that's about all we're going to do. We like them that way.

Tell me the truth… have you ever tried to eat boiled okra?

Yes, you say?

Well, now you know why we prefer it fried.

'Nough said.

There's an art and skill to the proper preparation and process of fried fresh vegetables. Here's some recipes to help you develop your skill.

FRIED SQUASH

6 – 8 medium sized yellow or zucchini squash – peeled and thinly sliced

1 egg, beaten

½ cup milk

½ cup all-purpose flour

½ cup cornmeal

1 pinch salt

1 pinch ground black pepper

1 pinch garlic salt

1 cup oil for frying

- Combine egg and milk together in a small bowl, mix well.
- In a second bowl, combine flour, cornmeal, salt, pepper and garlic salt. Dip squash slices first in the egg mixture, then dredge the squash in the dry mixture.
- Heat ½ inch of oil in a deep skillet over medium heat. Fry squash until golden brown on each side, turn and brown other side.
- Add more grease as needed.
- Remove and drain on paper towel

FRIED OKRA

3/4 cup cornmeal

3/4 cup flour

1 tsp. garlic powder

¼ tsp. salt

¼ tsp. pepper

½ cup buttermilk – (or make your own buttermilk by adding 1 TBSP vinegar to a measuring cup, fill with milk to make ½ cup, let sit 5 minutes)

2 lbs. okra, cut in 1/2 inch pieces

Oil for frying (start with 1 cup; add more if needed)

- In a cast iron skillet or deep pan, heat about 1 cup oil to about 350 degrees.
- Place cut okra in buttermilk to soak for a couple minutes while you assemble the coating mix.
- In a bowl, combine cornmeal, flour, and seasonings.
- Transfer okra to coating mixture and toss well to coat.
- Fry okra in hot oil for about 5 minutes, stirring to fry evenly.
- Remove to paper towels to drain.

FRIED POTATO CAKES

If you have mashed potatoes left over from another meal, this recipe is a delicious way to use them for another meal.

1 egg

1 cup mashed potatoes (left over)

1/3 cup flour

1 green onion (finely chopped)

½ tsp. baking powder

1 tsp. salt

¼ tsp. black pepper

1 -2 TBSP milk

2 -3 TBSPs shortening or vegetable oil

Beat the egg; mix the beaten egg with the mashed potatoes.

Stir in the dry ingredients.

Add the milk and mix well. The batter should be very thick.

Melt the shortening or heat the oil in a skillet.

Spoon batter into the skillet to form small pancakes, about ½ " thick.

Over medium heat, brown on one side, turn and brown on the other side.

NOTES:

POTATO SKILLET

"I have made a lot of mistakes falling in love, and regretted most of them, but never the potatoes that went with them. - Nora Ephron

---

1 Tbsp butter

1 Tbsp olive oil

4 russet potatoes, peeled and thinly sliced

salt and pepper to taste

1/8 tsp. cayenne pepper (optional)

1/4 tsp. paprika

2 tsp. McCormick brand Perfect Pinch garlic and herb , salt free seasoning mix

Salt and pepper to taste

*I use McCormick's Perfect Pinch seasoning mix because I rarely have fresh herbs in my kitchen. This recipe is especially tasty with fresh herbs. If you wish to use fresh herbs, use these measurements.:

1 tsp. chopped fresh rosemary

1Tbsp chopped fresh thyme

1 tsp. chopped fresh oregano

1 Tbsp chopped fresh flat-leaf parsley

1 ½ Tbsp minced garlic

- Melt the butter and heat the olive oil in a large skillet over medium heat.
- Arrange the potato slices across the bottom of the skillet in a single layer.
- Cook without stirring for 5 minutes, or until the potatoes have begun to brown on the bottom.
- Sprinkle potato slices with McCormick seasoning or with fresh rosemary, thyme, oregano, parsley, and paprika.
- Turn the potatoes, and continue cooking 5 minutes, or until tender.
- *If using fresh garlic, turn off the heat, and sprinkle the garlic and cayenne over the potatoes. Lightly toss for about 1 minute, until the garlic has softened.

BAKED SLICED POTATOES

4 large baking potatoes

¼ cup butter or margarine, melted

¼ cup vegetable oil

2 cloves garlic, minced

½ tsp – 1 tsp salt

½ tsp dried thyme leaves

- Wash potatoes well, then cut in ¼ inch –thick slices.
- Place overlapping slices in buttered 9x13 inch baking dish.
- Mix butter and oil. Brush slices with mixture first, then pour over potatoes.
- Sprinkle with garlic, salt and thyme
- Bake at 400 degrees for 25 – 30 minutes or until potatoes are done and browned at the edges.
- Serve immediately. Serves 4.

THREE CHEESE POTATO CASSEROLE

3 lbs. baking potatoes, peeled and quartered

½ cup butter or margarine

6 oz. cream cheese, softened

1 cup shredded cheddar cheese, divided

¾ cup finely chopped green pepper

¾ cup finely chopped green onions

½ cup grated Parmesan cheese

½ cup milk

1 tsp salt

- Cover potatoes in water in a large saucepan. Boil 15 minutes or until tender.
- Drain and mash potatoes.
- Add butter/margarine and cream cheese. Beat with electric mixer, medium speed until smooth.
- Stir in ½ cup cheddar cheese, green pepper, and remaining ingredients.
- Spoon mixture into lightly greased 9 x 13 baking dish.
- Bake uncovered at 350 degrees for 15 – 30 minutes or until thoroughly heated.
- Sprinkle with remaining cheddar cheese, bake additional 5 minutes or until cheese melts.

Makes 8 servings.

FRESH ASPARAGUS WITH ONION

> ***Life expectancy would grow by leaps and bounds if green vegetables smelled as good as bacon. – Doug Larsen***

There's no bacon in this recipe, but it's still pretty darn good.

1 Tbsp canola oil

1 Tbsp butter

1 small onion, chopped

1 cup chicken broth

1 lb. fresh asparagus

Salt

- Place oil, butter, and onion in medium pan over medium heat. Saute onion 3 minutes.
- Add broth and bring to a boil.
- Add asparagus, season with salt and cover pan.
- Lower heat and simmer about 8 minutes or until tender.

*You can substitute fresh green beans for asparagus. Cook beans about 15 – 20 minutes, or until tender.

SUNFLOWER SPINACH SALAD

3 cups iceberg lettuce, torn

3 cups romain lettuce, torn

1 cup fresh spinach, torn

4 hard-boiled eggs, sliced

1 (1 oz slice Swiss cheese, cut in julienne strips

1 (1 oz) slice Cheddar cheese, cut in julienne strips

¼ cup sunflower kernels, toasted

Red wine vinegar or café salad dressing (I use Kraft's red wine vinegar or Sweet Vidalia Onion salad dressing)

- Combine iceberg lettuce, romaine, and spinach in large bowl.
- Top with egg slices, cheese strips, and sunflower kernels.
- Serve with your choice of salad dressing.

*I have found that a tangy, sort of sweet dressing works well with this salad. It would be OK with Ranch, but I prefer the vinegary/sweet dressings. Thousand Island dressing would work if you prefer a creamy dressing.

GERMAN CUCUMBER SALAD

6 to 8 small pickling cucumbers

Salt

Vinegar

Pepper

Mayonnaise

Plain, unflavored & unsweetened, yogurt

- Peel cucumbers, slice paper thin.
- Place in bowl, sprinkle with a handful of salt.
- Let stand for about 1/2 hour.
- Then, by handfuls, squeeze out the excess water and put cucumbers in another bowl.
- To this, add 1 or 2 Tbsp vinegar, salt and pepper to taste.
- Add 1 heaping Tbsp mayonnaise and 1 heaping Tbsp yogurt.
- Lightly mix/toss mayonnaise and yogurt over cucumbers and let set for ½ hour or more before serving.

This is a recipe that my neighbor, Trudy, gave me. Trudy married an American serviceman and came to the U.S. from Germany as a young bride. She ended up in Wichita Falls, Texas. We sat on our adjoining front porches and talked about food and life a lot. I miss you, dear friend.

SOUR CREAM GERMAN CUCUMBER SALAD

2 large or 5 to 6 pickling cucumbers

1 tsp. salt

2 Tbsp sugar

1 Tbsp. white vinegar

½ cup sour cream

1 tsp dill, dry

1 tsp.paprika

- Peel cucumbers and slice very thin.
- Place cucumbers in colander and sprinkle with salt.
- Let stand 15-30 minutes.
- Squeeze liquid out of cucumbers.
- Whisk remaining ingredients and pour over cucumbers. Best if marinated for an hour or more.

SUMMER TOMATO, ONION, & CUCUMBER SALAD

A combination of fresh-from-the-garden tomatoes, onions, and cucumbers makes a delicious, healthy salad. Add some fresh or dried herbs and let this combination marinate for about an hour before serving.

3 Tbsp rice vinegar

1 Tbsp canola oil

1 tsp honey

½ tsp salt

½ tsp freshly ground pepper, or more to taste

2 medium cucumbers

4 medium tomatoes, cut into 1/2-inch wedges

1 Vidalia or other sweet onion, sliced thin

2 Tbsp coarsely chopped fresh herbs, such as flat-leaf parsley, chives and/or tarragon

*If using dried herbs, start with ½ tsp. and add to taste.

- Whisk vinegar, oil, honey, salt and pepper in a large shallow bowl.
- Peel cucumbers. Slice the cucumbers into thin rounds. Add the cucumber slices, tomatoes and onion slices to the dressing; gently toss to combine.
- Let stand at room temperature for at least 30 minutes and up to 1 hour.
- Add herbs just prior to serving and toss again to mix.

OLD FASHIONED CUCUMBER SALAD

2-3 med. cucumbers

1 med. onion

1 ½ tsp salt

¾ c. white vinegar

2 Tbsp. sugar

¼ tsp pepper

- Wash cucumbers. Do not peel. Score with tines of fork.
- Cut cucumbers and onion into transparent, paper thin slices to measure 4 to 5 cups.
- Whisk together salt, vinegar, sugar and pepper and pour over slices.
- Cover and refrigerate at least 4 hours; can be made the night before. Serve in a bowl or drain and serve on greens.

CARROT SALAD

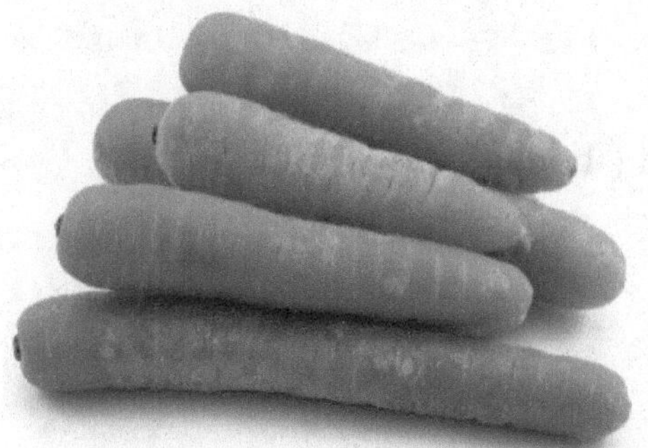

"Did you ever stop to taste a carrot? Not just eat it, but taste it? You can't taste the beauty and energy of the earth in a Twinkie." - Astrid Alauda –

4 large carrots (not baby carrots)

1 ripe, red mango

½ cup dried cranberries or craisins

¼ cup mayonnaise

- Wash carrots, peel and grate.
- Slice mango, then cut into cubes. Add to carrots. Add craisins.
- Add mayonnaise. Add more or less according to taste.
- Stir to lightly coat ingredients with mayonnaise. Refrigerate and let it set for 30 minutes so the flavors mingle together.

*This made a delicious, sweet salad complemented by the nutty taste of the carrots, the tartness of cranberries, and sweetness of the mango. The mayonnaise acted as a base and blended it all together. I did not add salt or sugar to this. The natural sweetness of the produce was all that was needed.
This recipe is easily adapted to use whatever you have in the refrigerator. To the grated carrots, just add crushed pineapple, coconut, diced apples, raisins or whatever you like.

Warm Red Cabbage Salad

3 Tbsp olive oil

1 medium red cabbage, shredded (about 4 cups)

2 Tbsp red wine vinegar

2 tsp. Dijon mustard

1/4 tsp ground pepper

¼ cup crumbled blue cheese (1oz)

3 bacon slices, cooked and crumbled

- In large nonstick skillet, heat oil over medium heat.
- Add cabbage; cook and stire 3 minutes or until slight wilted.
- Stir in vinegar, mustard and pepper. Cook 2 more minutes
- Transfer to large serving bowl.
- Top with blue cheese.

*Please see the note at the end of the book if you are worried by my spelling of blue cheese.

SHOE PEG CORN SALAD

1 (11 oz) can shoe peg corn, drained

1 (8 oz) can small early green peas, drained (I use Le Sueur brand)

1 (8 oz) can cut green beans, drained

1 cup chopped celery

½ cup chopped red onion

½ cup chopped green pepper

1 (2 oz) jar chopped pimiento, drained (optional)

*The pimiento makes the salad very colorful, but I hate pimiento peppers so I don't use them.

Dressing:

1/3 cup sugar

¼ cup vegetable oil

1/3 cup vinegar

1 tsp salt

- In large bowl, stir together all vegetables, set aside.
- In small saucepan, whisk together dressing ingredients. Heat over medium heat until sugar is melted.
- Pour over vegetables and chill overnight.

Makes 8 servings.

SOUTHERN SUMMER CHICKEN SALAD

2 boneless, skinless chicken breasts, cooked and diced

1 small can pineapple tidbits (drained and juice reserved

1 cup sliced fresh strawberries

1 cup thinly sliced celery

1 small (or ½ cup) sweet red onion, diced

3 or 4 fresh peaches, peeled, pitted and diced

Bag of baby spinach

1 cup chopped roasted pecans

2 to 3 Tbsp Miracle Whip

- Place first 6 ingredients in mixing bowl.
- Combine Miracle Whip and pineapple juice to make dressing. Use only enough juice to make a creamy dressing.
- Pour dressing over ingredients in bowl. Toss to coat.
- Serve on bed of spinach leaves. Top with pecans.

Makes 4 to 6 servings.

SALMON SALAD

1 can red salmon

1 apple, chopped

Sweet pickles to taste, chopped

Onions to taste, chopped

½ cup Miracle Whip salad dressing or mayonnaise

- Drain salmon in colander. Remove skin and bones.
- Flake salmon.
- Add apple, pickles, and onions and mix together lightly.
- Add salad dressing and mix gently, taking care not to make it mushy.
- Refrigerate for 2 hours before serving.
- Serve with crackers or crusty bread.

TUNA SALAD

2 small cans light or albacore tuna (water packed)

1 apple, chopped

2 boiled eggs, chopped

¼ cup onion, chopped

½ cup chopped sweet pickles

½ cup chopped pecans

Salad dressing or mayonnaise to taste

- Drain tuna, place in mixing bowl and flake apart.
- Add apple, eggs, onion, sweet pickles, and pecans.
- Mix and stir in salad dressing or mayonnaise until pleased with the consistency.

RANCH STYLE SALAD

1 15 oz. can Ranch Style Beans or chili beans (undrained)

1 cup diced or shredded Cheddar cheese

1 cup diced onions

½ head Iceburg lettuce (or lettuce of choice)

1 large tomato

2 Tbsp French dressing

Corn chips (I use Fritos)

*Do not drain beans, the juice adds to the flavor.

- Place all ingredients, except corn chips, in a large salad bowl.
- Mix well. Refrigerate for a few hours to allow flavors to mix.
- Add corn chips to mixture just prior to serving.

*Chips will become soggy if added too soon.

MEXICAN CHEF SALAD

1 head lettuce, chopped

4 tomatoes, chopped

2 avocados, sliced

1 cup grated cheese

1 onion, chopped

7 oz. can pinto beans, drained

1 (8 oz.) bottle Catalina dressing

1 pkg. tortilla chips, broken

- Brown and drain ground meat.
- While still warm, mix with other ingredients.
- Add tortilla chips and serve.

* Tortilla chips can be added to the salad or served separately. They will become soggy if left over.

MACARONI SALAD

1 16 oz. pkg. shell macaroni

1 bell pepper, diced

1 small purple onion, diced

2 carrots, shredded

6 boiled eggs, chopped

1 cup sweet pickles, diced

Salt and pepper to taste

Salad dressing or mayonnaise (to taste)

- Boil macaroni as directed, drain, and set aside to cool.
- Mix all other ingredients together (except salad dressing).
- Add macaroni and salad dressing, tossing all ingredients together lightly.
- Refrigerate for at least one hour before serving.

SOUR CREAM MANDARIN FRUIT SALAD

1 (11 oz.) can mandarin oranges, drained

1 (20 oz.) can pineapple chunks, drained

1 (10 oz.) jar maraschino cherries, drained

1 cup of mini marshmallows (unflavored)

1 cup flaked coconut

1 cup sour cream

- Drain the oranges, pineapple and cherries well. (Reserve juices for another use if you like.)
- Combine the fruit with the marshmallows and coconut; toss to mix.
- Fold in the sour cream, cover and chill several hours or until ready to serve.

PINK STUFF

1 (24 oz) can -cherry pie filling

1 (14 oz) can sweetened condensed milk

1(8oz) can crushed pineapple (drained)

1 bag Mini Marshmallows

1 cup chopped pecans (optional)

24 oz tub Cool Whip

*Use a large mixing bowl to mix this.

*Drain crushed pineapple thoroughly by placing in colander or sieve and mashing with spoon . (too much juice will cause the mixture to separate)

- Next combine all ingredients except the Cool Whip and the cherry pie filling. Mix well.
- Fold in the cherry pie filling and then fold in the Cool Whip.
- Refrigerate overnight before serving.

*But, be sure you lick the spoon so you can get a preview taste of this yummy pink stuff!

FRESH APPLE SALAD

¾ cup mayonnaise or salad dressing

1 Tbsp plus 2 tsp. lemon juice

1 Tbsp plus 2 tsp. milk

3 medium unpeeled apples, coarsely chopped (3 cups)

3 medium celery stalks, chopped (1 ½ cups)

½ cup coarsely chopped nuts

Salad greens, if desired

- Mix mayonnaise, lemon juice and milk in medium bowl.
- Stir in apples, celery and nuts. Let sit for at least 30 minutes before serving.
- Serve on salad greens.

Chapter 6:
Cornbread and Biscuits

"The best comfort food will always be greens, cornbread, and fried chicken."
- Maya Angelou -

Eating warm, fresh cornbread crumbled into a glass of cold fresh milk is perhaps an acquired taste. But it was something my family enjoyed.

When I queried my cousins about recipes they wanted to contribute to this book, each of them mentioned their memories of eating cornbread and sweet milk at their grandparents' house.

It was a simpler time. We personally knew the source of our milk; she had a name. One of our milk sources was a Jersey cow named Betsy.

Milk was stored in a crockery pitcher, not in a plastic milk jug. And it was replenished each morning and evening when my Mama milked the cow.

Cornbread was baked in a cast iron skillet and served with home churned butter. Mama skimmed the cream off the top of the milk and put in a Mason jar. My job was shaking the jar until the cream turned into butter.

There are different ways to prepare cornbread. Some people prefer it made with buttermilk; others prefer a hint of sweetness. Some cooks add bacon grease to the mix, some cooks use lard to grease their skillet, and some add butter.

It has been a long time since I have eaten cornbread crumbled in a glass of unpasteurized, non-homogenized milk, but I savor the memory of being a little girl watching my Daddy pour milk in a jelly glass and mash up his last slice of cornbread in it.

Then he would shake a little salt in it, grab a spoon, and share it with me.

I like my cornbread to be moist in the center, with no added sugar. I eat it slathered with butter that I buy at the grocery store now.

I like cornbread served with beans, greens, and ham. Or with fried chicken. Or all by itself, straight out of the skillet.

And then of course, there's always the option of eating it with a glass of cold, sweet milk.

.

BUTTERMILK CORNBREAD

1 cup plain yellow cornmeal

1 cup all-purpose flour

1 TBSP baking powder

1 tsp. salt

¼ tsp. baking soda

2 cups buttermilk

2 large eggs

½ cup butter

- Preheat oven to 425°.
- Whisk together first 5 ingredients in a large bowl.
- Whisk together buttermilk and eggs; stir into cornmeal mixture just until combined.
- Heat a 10-inch cast-iron skillet over medium-high heat until it just begins to smoke. Add butter, and stir until butter is melted.
- Stir melted butter into cornbread batter. Pour batter into hot skillet.
- Bake at 425° for 25 to 30 minutes or until golden and cornbread pulls away from sides of skillet.
- Invert cornbread onto a wire rack or a plate; serve warm.

SWEET CORNBREAD

1 ¼ cup all-purpose flour

1 cup plus 3 TBSP plain white cornmeal

¼ cup sugar

1 TBSP baking powder

1 tsp. salt

¼ cup butter, melted

2 large eggs

1 cup milk

- Preheat oven to 400°.
- Lightly grease an 8-inch cast-iron skillet, and heat in oven 5 minutes.
- Meanwhile, whisk together first 5 ingredients in a bowl; whisk in melted butter.
- Add eggs and milk, whisking just until smooth.
- Pour batter into hot skillet. Bake at 400° for 30 to 33 minutes or until golden brown.

MEXICAN CORNBREAD

½ cup butter, melted

¾ cup white sugar

4 eggs

1 (15 ounce) cans cream-style corn

2 small cans chopped green chili peppers, drained

½ cup shredded Monterey Jack cheese

½ cup shredded Cheddar cheese

1 cup all-purpose flour

1 cup yellow cornmeal

¼ tsp. salt

4 tsp. baking powder

- Preheat oven to 300 degrees Fahrenheit . Lightly grease a 9x13 inch baking dish.
- In a large bowl, beat together butter and sugar. Beat in eggs one at a time.
- Blend in cream corn, peppers, and cheese.
- In a separate bowl, stir together flour, cornmeal, baking powder and salt.
- Add flour mixture to corn mixture; stir until smooth.
- Pour batter into prepared pan.
- Bake in preheated oven for 1 hour, until a toothpick inserted into center of the pan comes out clean.

HUSH PUPPIES

1 cup yellow cornmeal

¼ cup all-purpose flour

1 ½ tsp. baking powder

½ tsp. salt

1 egg, lightly beaten

¾ cup milk

1 small onion, finely chopped

Oil for deep-fat frying

- Combine the cornmeal, flour, baking powder, and salt in a large bowl.
- In a separate bowl, whisk the egg, milk and onion; add to dry ingredients just until combined.
- In a deep-fat fryer or electric skillet, heat oil to 365°.
- Drop batter by teaspoonfuls into oil. Fry 2 to 2 ½ minutes or until golden brown.
- Drain on paper towels. Serve warm.
- *Hush Puppies are a good addition to a fried fish dinner, but they are also perfect with a bowl of slow-cooked pinto beans or chili beans.

CORNBREAD SALAD

1 pan cornbread (see recipe here or use a package of cornbread mix)

1 cup diced onions

1 bell pepper, seeded and diced

1 cup diced fresh tomatoes

15 oz can whole kernel corn, drained

1 lb. bacon, cooked until crisp and crumbled

2-3 cups mayonnaise (I used two)

1 pkg. (1 oz) dry ranch dressing mix

- Bake cornbread. Cool and crumble and place in large bowl.
- Add in onions, bell pepper, diced tomatoes, corn,and bacon.
- Stir until well combined.
- In a separate bowl, place mayonnaise and ranch mix (if using ranch mix, optional) Stir until well blended.
- Add mayonnaise mixture to salad and stir until fully mixed. Cover and refrigerate at least two hours before serving.

*This recipe makes a huge amount of salad. It is perfect for taking to potluck suppers and holiday gatherings.

NOTES:

"Cooking is one failure after another, and that's how you finally learn."

~ Julia Child

I have been cooking for a long time… like for forty-five years. Only recently did I learn to make perfect biscuits.

Oh, I've tried for a long time to make perfect biscuits… like for forty-five years. But, I just couldn't get the hang of it.

I watched Mama bake biscuits. She simply sifted this and that and poured in a little buttermilk and grease , kneaded it with her hands and rolled it out with her old rolling pin. She made perfect biscuits.

I tried doing that. But it didn't work for me.

At my wedding shower, I received a pastry blender and I couldn't wait to use it to cut shortening in to a mound of flour. It worked for my pie crusts, but not so much for my biscuits. Come to think of it, my pie crusts weren't that great either.

I tried using biscuit mix … Bisquick…Martha White … Bis-Kits…you name it…and still turned out little flat biscuits that tasted fine, but looked like toasty brown hockey pucks.

My biscuits were ugly. And I just wanted a biscuit I could be proud of. . I felt like a failure… at least concerning biscuit baking.

I resorted to baking frozen biscuits. And sometimes, I must confess, I baked some canned biscuits.

The only real stumbling block is fear of failure. In cooking you've got to have a what-the-hell attitude."

~ Julia Child

And then…I moved to Oklahoma. And I bought some Shawnee Mills flour.

I said… "What the hell" and gave biscuit making another try.

And… I made my first perfect biscuits by using Shawnee Mills flour and the recipe printed on the back side of the flour sack.

HOMESTEAD BISCUITS

2 cups all purpose flour (I used Shawnee Best All Purpose Flour)

4 tsp baking powder

1 tsp salt

3 Tbsp shortening

¾ to 1 cup milk

Preheat oven to 450 degrees.
Lightly grease a baking sheet or pan. I use a pie pan.

- Sift together flour, baking powder, salt.
- Cut in shortening until like coarse crumbs.
- Add milk and mix lightly to make a soft dough.
- Knead lightly on floured surface and roll to ½ inch thickness.
- Cut dough to desired size and place on a light greased baking sheet or pan with sices touching
- Bake at 450 degrees for 10-12 minutes.

Makes 18 two inch biscuits.
*I don't have a biscuit cutter, so I turn a jelly glass upside down and use that to cut my biscuits. It's just the right size.

SHAWNEE CHEESE BREAD

4 ¾ - 5 ¼ all purpose flour (I use Shawnee Best All Purpose Flour… because it works for me.)

2 tsp baking powder

2 tsp salt

2 Tbsp sugar

2 packages dry active yeast

¾ cup water

1 ¼ cups buttermilk

2 Tbsp margarine or butter

1 cup coarsely shredded Cheddar cheese

1 egg, slightly beaten

1 Tbsp milk

- Mix 1 ½ cups flour, sugar, salt, baking powder and yeast.
- Heat buttermilk, water and margarine/butter in sauce pan on low until liquids are very warm (120 – 130 degrees)
- Slowly add to dry ingredients; use electric mixer and beat 2 minutes at medium speed.
- Add 1 cup flour.
- Beat at high speed 2 minutes.
- Stir in cheese and enough flour for a stiff dough.
- Place on lightly floured surface; knead until smooth and elastic (7-10 minutes).
- Divide dough and shape into 2 round loaves.
- Place on greased baking sheets.
- Cover and let rise in warm place until doubled (about 1 hour)
- Mix egg and milk; brush on loaves.
- Bake at 350 degrees for 40-45 minutes. Cool on wire racks.

Now that you have biscuits, it's time to make the gravy.

> ***"I come from a family where gravy is considered a beverage." - Erma Bombeck -***

SOUTHERN SAUSAGE GRAVY

1 pound bulk pork sausage

¼ cup all-purpose flour

2 cups milk (2% or whole)

Salt and black pepper to taste

Hot biscuits, of course

- Warm a large skillet over medium heat. Add the sausage and break into chunks with a spatula (I use a potato masher).
- Cook until the meat is crumbled and browned all the way through.
- Add the flour by sprinkling it over the hot sausage and cook until dissolved, about 1 minute.
- Stir in the milk.
- Cook, whisking frequently, until the gravy is very thick and bubbly (you can add more milk later if you need to thin).
- Season generously with salt and lots of freshly ground black pepper.

Serve with hot biscuits.

CHOCOLATE GRAVY

1 ½ cups sugar

2 ½ Tbsp flour

2 ½ Tbsp cocoa

1½ cups milk

½ cup water

A few drops of vanilla (optional)

- Mix sugar, flour and cocoa in a large skillet then add the water to mix.
- Add the milk and cook on medium heat until thick.
- Add the few drops of vanilla while cooking (optional)
- Serve over hot buttered biscuits

Chapter 7: Cakes

"I always say a little prayer when I put cakes in the oven," remarked Eve, as she stopped to kiss Rose good-bye.
"What do you say?"
"I say, 'Please, God, don't let me forget I've put that cake in the oven."
— Hilary McKay

I received my first and only Bundt cake pan as a wedding present in 1975. As I write this book, my cake pan and I have been faithful partners for 40 years and I expect to celebrate a golden anniversary someday.

I no longer have the original husband, but I still have my original avocado colored Bundt pan. Well, you know…when you find a good cake pan, you need to hang on to it.

The Bundt pan was a relatively new design in cookware in 1975…just as I was a relatively new cook. It was designed by H. David Dalquist and it exploded in popularity when it was used by a Texas housewife to bake a cake for a Pillsbury Bake-Off.

My wedding present allowed me to explore a whole new aspect of cooking. Having my own cookware and a kitchen of my own to use it in was like having the playhouse I had dreamed of as a little girl. Instead of stirring up a batch of mud-pies, I could bake real cakes and pies.

It was great fun learning to cook and bake.

With my Bundt pan, I could bake all manner of cakes and when I turned them out of the pan, they looked rather elegant due to the design of the pan. All I had to do was to add an icing or glaze and pour it over the top of the warm cake.

Ta da! I had a beautiful cake, ready to take to a church supper. If I didn't burn it to a crisp first.

One of the first cakes I baked in my Bundt pan was the Tunnel of Fudge Cake. It became my "specialty".

The Tunnel of Fudge Cake was invented by Ella Helfrich. She entered it in the 17th annual Pillsbury Bake-Off and won second place.

Mrs. Helfrich's recipe had only 6 ingredients, one of which made the delicious gooey tunnel in the center of the cake…the tunnel of fudge. Mrs. Helfrich's original formula required the Pillsbury Dutch Chocolate frosting mix for the inside.

I baked the Tunnel of Fudge Cake to good reviews from my friends and family until the day the unthinkable happened. Yes, Pillsbury stopped making the Dutch chocolate frosting mix called for in the recipe.

It was a sad day for me. It must have been a sad day for a lot of other bakers, too, because Pillsbury revised the recipe and re-issued it without the Dutch Chocolate frosting.

Here is the revised recipe, word for word, from the Pillsbury website, www.pillsbury.com

TUNNEL OF FUDGE CAKE

1 ¾ cups sugar

1 ¾ cups margarine or butter, softened

6 eggs

2 cups powdered sugar

2 ¼ cups Pillsbury BEST® All Purpose Flour (or whatever you want)

¾ cup unsweetened cocoa

*2 cups chopped walnuts or pecans

GLAZE

¾ cup powdered sugar

¼ cup unsweetened cocoa

4 to 6 tsp milk

- Heat oven to 350°F.
- Grease and flour 12-cup Bundt pan or 10-inch tube pan.
- In large bowl, combine sugar and margarine; beat until light and fluffy.
- Add eggs one at a time, beating well.
- Gradually add 2 cups powdered sugar; blend well.
- By hand, stir in flour and remaining cake ingredients until well blended. S
- Spoon batter into greased and floured pan; spread evenly.
- Bake at 350°F for 45 to 50 minutes or until top is set and edges are beginning to pull away from edge of pan.
- Cool upright in pan on wire rack 1 ½ hours; invert onto serving plate. Cool for at least 2 hours more.
- In small bowl, combine all glaze ingredients, adding enough milk for desired drizzling consistency.
- Spoon over top of cake, allowing some to run down sides. Store tightly covered.

*Nuts are essential for the success of this recipe.

**Since this cake has a soft filling, an ordinary doneness test cannot be used. Accurate oven temperature and baking times are essential.

NOTES:

More Cakes that Work Well in a Bundt Pan

SOUR CREAM CAKE

2 sticks butter

3 cups sugar

6 eggs. Separated

3 cups sifted flour

¼ tsp salt

¼ tsp soda

1 tsp vanilla

1 cup sour cream

- Grease and flour a tube or Bundt pan. Set oven at 350 degrees (F).
- Sift flour and soda together 3 times. Set aside
- Cream butter and sugar together. Add vanilla.
- Add one egg yolk at a time to creamed mixture, beating well after each addition.
- Add salt to egg whites. Beat egg whites until they form a peak.
- Alternate adding the flour and soda with sour cream to the creamed butter and sugar.
- Beat until thoroughly blended.
- Gently fold in beaten egg whites.
- Turn batter in to greased and floured pan. Bake 1 hour or until done.

POUND CAKE

2 sticks butter

2 cups sugar

6 eggs

2 cups flour

1 tsp. vanilla

- Cream butter well, gradually add sugar and beat after each addition.
- Add eggs, one at a time, beating well after each addition. Add vanilla.
- *The first steps may be done with an electric mixer, but flour must be folded in gradually by hand.
- Sift flour, measure and add by folding in a little at a time by hand.
- Grease and flour 10 inch tube cake pan. Pour in batter and bake at 350 degrees for about 45 minutes.
- Cool before removing from pan. No icing is needed.

GERMAN CHOCOLATE POUND CAKE

2 cups sugar

1 cup butter

4 eggs

2 tsp. vanilla

½ tsp. salt

1 tsp. soda

1 cup buttermilk

3 cups sifted flour

1 pkg. German sweet chocolate

- Cream sugar and butter together.
- Add eggs, vanilla, and buttermilk.
- Add flour, soda, and salt. Mix well.
- Soften chocolate in a warm oven. Add softened chocolate to the mixture.
- Blend together well.
- Spoon batter in to greased and floured Bundt pan.
- Bake about 1 ½ hours in 300 degree oven.
- Remove cake from the pan while still hot.
- Place under a tight fitting cake cover and leave covered until thoroughly cooled.

The Church Ladies

One of the best things about attending church is the gathering of the faithful in the fellowship hall to break bread together. There are other benefits, of course, but this is my favorite one.

Not only did the Church Ladies provide a bountiful spread of delicious casseroles, salads, desserts, and breads they fed us all with encouragement and love.

I have rarely felt more loved than when I was cooking and eating with my friends, the faithful Church Ladies. Precious memories, how they linger…how they ever flood my soul.

> ***And they devoted themselves to the apostles' teaching and the fellowship, to the breaking of bread and the prayers. Acts 2:42***

HAWAIIAN HUKULAI CAKE

2 cups flour

2 tsp. soda

2 tsp. cinnamon

1 ½ tsp. salt

2 cups sugar

4 eggs, slightly beaten

1 ½ cup vegetable oil

1 – 8 oz. can crushed pineapple and juice

1 cup chopped nuts

2 cups shredded carrots

½ cup chopped dates

1 cup flaked coconut

- Sift flour, soda, cinnamon and salt together; set aside
- Combine sugar, eggs and oil.
- Add oil mixture to flour mixture, blending well.
- Add remaining ingredients; mix well.
- Spoon batter into greased and floured 10 inch Bundt pan.
- Bake in preheated 350 degree oven for hour or until cake tests done.
- Frost after cake has cooled.

FROSTING:

1 cup confectioners sugar

¼ cup butter or margarine

1 – 3 oz. package cream cheese, softened

1 tsp. vanilla

FRESH APPLE CAKE

3 cups sifted flour

1 tsp. baking soda

½ tsp. salt

1 tsp. cinnamon

1 cup cooking oil

2 cups sugar

2 eggs

2 tsp. vanilla

3 cups chopped fresh apples

- Preheat oven to 325 degrees. Grease and flour bundt or tube pan.
- Sift together flour, baking soda, salt and cinnamon.
- In large mixing bowl combine cooking oil and sugar, cream thoroughly.
- Add eggs and vanilla and continue beating until light and fluffy.
- Add sifted dry ingredients and apples and mix until just thoroughly blended.
- Pour in to pan and bake for 1 hour 15 minutes at 325 degrees.

MAMA'S NO-BAKE CHEESE CAKE

1 box lemon Jello

1 cup hot water

¾ cup sugar

1 lemon

1 tsp. grated lemon rind

½ tsp. vanilla

1 8oz. package of cream cheese

1 large can evaporated milk

4-5 TBSP melted butter

20-24 graham crackers

- Mix Jello, hot water and ½ cup sugar together.
- Chill in refrigerator until partially congealed.
- Mix ¼ cup sugar, vanilla, juice of 1 lemon and grated lemon rind with the whole package of cream cheese.
- Chill and whip evaporated milk; add Jello mixture and beat.
- Add cream cheese mixture.

CRUST:

- Mix melted butter with graham crackers, 9 x 13 pan or two pie pans with crust.
- Pour the cheese cake mixture over the crust.
- Sprinkle a few cracker crumbs over the top, then decorate with cherries if desired.
- Chill overnight.

NOTES:

PINEAPPLE CHIFFON CAKE

2 ¼ cups sifted cake flour

1 ½ cups sugar

3 tsp. baking powder

1 tsp. salt

½ cup cooking oil

4 egg yolks

¾ cup unsweetened pineapple juice

1 cup or 8 egg whites

½ sp. Cream of tartar

- Sift dry ingredients into mixing bowl; make a well in center of dry ingredients.
- Add (in this order): oil, egg yolks, and pineapple juice. Beat this mixture until satin smooth. Set aside.
- Next combine egg whites and cream of tartar in large mixing bowl. Beat to very stiff peaks.
- Pour egg yolk batter in thin stream over entire sugar of beaten egg whites, gently cutting and folding just enough to blend.
- Pour in to ungreased 10 inch tube pan.
- ****Bake at 325 degrees for 55 minutes, then increase temperature to 350 degrees and bake 20 more minutes.***

- Remove from oven. Invert tube pan on cooling rack. Let cool before removing from pan.

*This is a delicious cake without icing, but it can be iced if you like.

PINEAPPLE BUTTER FROSTING

½ cup butter or oleo

4 cups sifted powdered sugar

¼ cup pineapple juice (or less…use just enough to make soft icing)

- Cream the butter/oleo with powdered sugar.
- Add enough pineapple juice to make a soft icing.
- Spread icing over cake after cake has cooled.

ANGEL FOOD CAKE

1 cup sifted cake flour

1 ½ cups sifted granulated sugar

1 ¼ cups (10 – 12) egg whites (at room temperature)

1 ¼ tsp. cream of tartar

¼ tsp. salt

1 tsp. vanilla extract

¼ tsp. almond extract

- Sift flour and ½ cup sugar together 3 times.
- Place egg whites in large mixing bowl and beat at high until all egg whites are foamy.
- Add cream of tartar, salt and flavoring.
- Beat at high until mixture stands in definite peaks, 2-3 minutes.
- Sift flour-sugar mixture evenly over egg white mixture about ¼ cup at a time.
- With rubber scraper, fold egg whites in lightly but thoroughly after each addition.
- Pour into ungreased 10 inch tube pan. Smooth top of batter carefully in pan.
- Bake in oven 350 degrees for 40 – 45 minutes. Invert pan and cool cake in pan for 1 hour or until cold before removing.

CRUNCHY APRICOT CAKE

1 – 22 oz. can apricot pie filling

1 pkg. white cake mix

1/3 cup water

1 egg

½ cup flaked coconut

½ cup chopped pecans

½ cup butter or margarine, melted

- Spread pie filling in bottom of 9 x 9 baking dish.
- Combine cake mix, water, and egg. Beat 4 minutes with electric mixer at medium speed.
- Pour over pie filling; sprinkle with coconut and pecans.
- Drizzle butter across top.
- Bake at 350 degrees for 40 minutes.

RED VELVET CAKE AND UNEXPECTED ACTS OF KINDNESS

From Left: Aunt Durelle, Cousin Gail, Aunt Ethel Martin, Grandma Martin, Cousin Sandra, Aunt Elizabeth

"Food is symbolic of love when words are inadequate." - Alan D. Wolfelt -

---

Our family could count on certain desserts on certain holidays each year. Thanksgiving, Christmas, and Easter all had their designated sweets that reflected the season.

Thanksgiving always found red velvet cake with seven minute frosting on the dessert table. While my mother had her own specialties, her sisters had theirs, too.

The red velvet cake was my Aunt Durelle's specialty. It was three layers of deliciousness, each separated by a special, secret filling, and encased by stiff, white, seven-minute frosting. Her cake defined the festive atmosphere of the holidays.

Of course, no recipe remains for that cake. The younger generation of cooks has tried to replicate it, but with little success.

My mother and aunts weren't ones to shout "Happy Holidays!" But like the women of their time, they spoke their love through cooking. The generous spread of food at our table told me that we were all well loved.

Now at the holidays, I remember the desserts and the love shared at our table with family who are now long gone, but always remembered.

At Thanksgiving a couple of years ago, I was working at a bookstore instead of sitting with my family around a table strained by its load of holiday desserts.

At my lunch break, I hurried to one of the only fast food restaurants that was open on Thanksgiving to catch a quick bite. On my way there, I reminisced about past holidays in general, and my aunt's red velvet cake, specifically.

I missed my parents and all my aunts and uncles. I missed our family gatherings.

I wished I could revisit those days if only for a few moments.

While I placed my order for a burger and fries, a family entered the restaurant and stood behind me, looking at the menu displayed on the wall. Grandparents, parents, and four kids ranging in age from about 11 to 18, waited patiently to place their order.

I noticed the mother was carrying a covered metal cake pan.

When I got my order, I found a booth and sat alone. I watched the family from the corner of my eye, while I silently ate my burger and read the newspaper. They spread out among three booths: eating, talking, and laughing.

After they finished their meal and cleared their table, the youngest child stood, smiling, beside his grandfather. The rest of the family gathered round and sang "Happy Birthday" to the boy.

Then the mother removed the lid from the cake pan, cut the cake and handed pieces to her family. She looked at me and said, "Would you like a piece of homemade red velvet cake?"

"Why, yes," I said. "Yes I would LOVE a piece of homemade red velvet cake."

She didn't know how much that slice of cake meant to me.

Or maybe she did.

After she gave me my slice, the woman proceeded to give a piece of love…er, cake…to everyone in the restaurant.

I knew only the barest of facts about the family. They told me they were travelling to a basketball tournament and had to be on the road on Thanksgiving Day and the little boy's birthday. So they brought their cake and their family traditions with them.

I never knew their names, but I will remember they shared their food and love with me and that is enough to know them by.

This is not my Aunt Durelle's recipe. That has never been found by any of us although we have searched through recipe boxes, shoe boxes, cookbooks, dresser drawers, and letters. We found no clues about the special filling she put between the layers.

However…I use this recipe and the recipe for the icing and it's the best alternative I have found. The cake is moist and delicious. The frosting is ***mahvelous, dahling***…

Red velvet cake has a delicate flavor although it is a hearty looking cake. Cream cheese frosting overpowers the taste of the cake. But this frosting, sometimes called Ermine Icing, is also delicate and is the perfect complement to the cake.

RED VELVET CAKE

½ cup Crisco

1 ½ cup sugar

2 oz. red food color

2 eggs

2 cups flour

1 tsp. salt

1 Tbsp cocoa

1 cup buttermilk

1 Tbsp vinegar

1tsp. soda

- Cream Crisco and sugar. Beat well.
- Add eggs and red food color.
- Mix in dry ingredients alternately with buttermilk.
- Dissolve soda in vinegar. Fold into mixture gently.
- DO NOT mix or beat after adding soda mixture.
- Bake at 350 degrees until it springs back at touch.

ICING:

1 tsp. salt

¼ cup flour

1 cup margarine or butter

1 small can of coconut (optional)

1 cup milk

1 cup sugar

2 tsp. vanilla

- Mix flour, salt and milk in a saucepan.
- Cook over low heat until smooth, thick and creamy. Cool completely.
- Cream sugar & margarine/butter together
- Cream cooled milk mixture with the sugar/butter mixture. Add vanilla and coconut to mixture.
- Spread on cooled cake.

NOTES:

Chapter 8: Cookies

"I want to take all our best moments, put them in a jar, and take them out like cookies and savor each one of them forever."
— Crystal Woods, Write like no one is reading

"A COOKIE AND A KISS"

A house should have a cookie jar

For when it's half past three

And children hurry home from school

As hungry as can be,

There's nothing quite so splendid

In filling children up

As spicy, fluffy ginger cakes

And sweet milk in a cup.

A house should have a mother

Waiting with a hug

No matter what the boy brings home

A puppy or a bug.

Author Unknown

Cookies are made of butter and love – Norwegian Proverb

My Granny Browning had a sweet tooth. She loved watermelon; she loved cookies, and she loved cold Coca-Cola in the little 6 ounce bottles. When you spent an afternoon with Granny, she fed you some cookies and Coke. In the summertime, she added watermelon.

Granny had an old cookie jar on her kitchen counter and she and my Aunt Fern kept it filled with her old-fashioned tea cakes. They were lightly sweet, had a little taste of baking soda, and were slightly burned around the edges.

When I was a little girl I liked to think the cookie jar was filled daily just for me, but even then I knew that all little girls and boys with dirt smudged faces and grimy hands were welcome to reach inside it to retrieve a sweet treasure.

"There's nothing quite so splendid" as the cookies and the love inside your grandmother's cookie jar. My Granny's cookie jar was always full of both.

Granny's Old Fashioned Tea Cakes

1 cup butter

1 ¾ cups white sugar

2 eggs

3 cups all-purpose flour

1/2 tsp baking soda

1/2 tsp salt

1/4 tsp ground nutmeg

1 teaspoon vanilla extract

Preheat the oven to 325 degrees.

- In a medium bowl, cream together the butter and sugar until smooth.
- Beat in the eggs one at a time, then stir in the vanilla.
- In a separate bowl, combine the flour, baking soda, salt and nutmeg; stir in to the creamed mixture.
- Place dough on a lightly floured board or wax paper; knead dough for a few turns.
- Cover and refrigerate until firm.
- On a lightly floured surface, roll the dough out to 1/4 inch in thickness.
- Cut into desired shapes with cookie cutters. Place cookies 1½ inches apart on cookie sheets.
- Bake for 8 to 10 minutes in the preheated oven.

Allow cookies to cool on baking sheet for 5 minutes before removing to a wire rack to cool completely.

SNICKERDOODLES

Snickerdoodles are lots of fun to make when you have little helpers around. There's lots of rolling up and rolling the dough in sugar and cinnamon. Be patient and have fun.

2 ¾ cups flour

2 tsp. cream of tartar

1 tsp baking soda

1 ¾ cups sugar, divided

½ cup butter, softened

½ cup shortening

2 eggs

2 tsp Vanilla extract

1 Tbsp cinnamon, ground

Preheat oven to 400°F.

- Mix flour, cream of tartar and baking soda in medium bowl. Set aside. Beat 1 1/2 cups of the sugar, butter and shortening in large bowl with electric mixer on medium speed until light and fluffy.
- Add eggs and vanilla; mix well.
- Gradually beat in flour mixture on low speed until well mixed. Refrigerate 1 hour.
- Mix remaining 1/4 cup sugar and cinnamon.
- Shape dough into 1-inch balls.
- Roll in cinnamon sugar mixture to coat.
- Place 2 inches apart on baking sheets.
- Bake 9 to 11 minutes or until lightly browned.
- Cool on baking sheets 1 minute.
- Remove to wire racks; cool completely.

GINGER SNAPS

2 cups flour

2 tsp baking soda

½ tsp salt

1 Tbsp ground ginger

1 tsp ground cinnamon

¾ cup shortening

1 cup sugar

¼ cup molasses

1 egg

Additional sugar, for rolling

Preheat oven to 350°F.

- Mix flour, baking soda, salt and spices in medium bowl. Set aside. Beat shortening and sugar in large bowl with electric mixer on medium speed until light and fluffy.
- Beat in molasses and egg.
- Gradually stir in flour mixture until well mixed.
- Shape dough into 1-inch balls. Roll in additional sugar to coat.
- Place 2 inches apart on ungreased baking sheets.
- Bake 12 minutes.
- Cool on baking sheets 1 minute.
- Remove to wire racks; cool completely.

Store in airtight container.

BROWN SUGAR COOKIES

1 cup margarine or butter

1 cup white sugar

1 cup brown sugar

2 eggs

1 tsp. vanilla

4 cups flour

1 tsp. baking soda

½ tsp. salt

- Cream oleo with sugars until light and fluffy, add eggs and vanilla then mix well.
- Sift flour, soda, and salt together.
- Gradually add flour mixture to creamed mixture, beating after each addition.
- Roll into rolls. Wrap in wax paper.
- Chill the rolls about 30 minutes. After chilling, you can cut in slices and place on ungreased baking sheet.
- Bake at 350 degrees for 8 to 12 minutes.

NO BAKE CHOCOLATE PEANUT BUTTER OATMEAL COOKIES

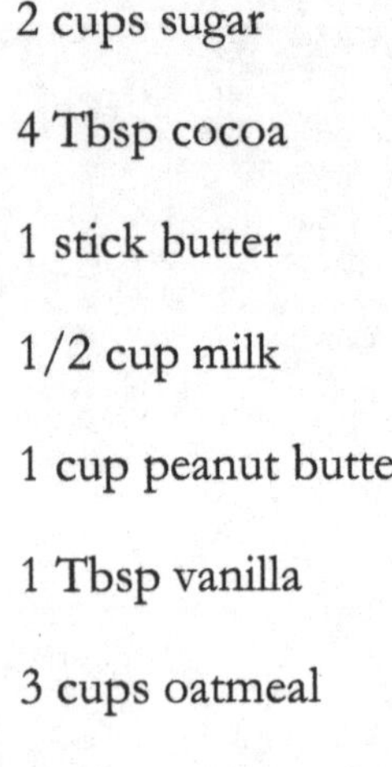

2 cups sugar

4 Tbsp cocoa

1 stick butter

1/2 cup milk

1 cup peanut butter

1 Tbsp vanilla

3 cups oatmeal

Waxed paper

- In a heavy saucepan bring the sugar, cocoa, butter and milk to a boil.
- Let boil for 1 minute then add peanut butter, vanilla and oatmeal.
- Stir to combine ingredients.
- On a sheet of waxed paper, drop mixture by the teaspoonfuls.
- Allow to cool and harden before eating.

NO BAKE PEANUT BUTTER KRISPIE COOKIES

1 cup sugar

1 cup corn syrup

1 1/3 cup creamy peanut butter

4 ¼ cups Rice Krispies cereal

½ cup chocolate chips (optional)

- In a large sauce pan over medium heat, melt the sugar, corn syrup, and peanut butter until smooth and evenly combined.
- Remove from heat.
- Quickly add cereal and stir to combine thoroughly.
- Add chocolate chips and stir again.
- Drop rounded tablespoons on to wax paper.

Let cool before eating.

EASY PEANUT BUTTER COOKIES

1 cup peanut butter

1 egg

1/3 cup water

1 box yellow cake mix

- Place peanut butter, egg, water, and one half of dry cake mix in large mixing bowl.
- Mix thoroughly.
- Add remaining dry mix, mixing with a wooden spoon.
- Roll into 1 inch balls with hands.
- Place on ungreased baking sheet, 2- 3 inches apart. Flatten with fork dipped into flour.
- Bake at 375 degrees for 8 – 10 minutes.
- Cool 1 – 2 minutes before removing from pan.

Makes about 5 dozen cookies.

EASY CREAM CHEESE COOKIES WITH STRAWBERRY FILLING

1 pkg Betty Crocker sugar cookie mix

Jello cheesecake pudding

1/3 cup oil

1 egg

Strawberry preserves

- Place cookie mix and pudding mix in mixing bowl.
- Add egg and oil and mix together.
- Roll dough into balls. Place on ungreased cookie sheet.
- Mash ball with thumb, making a thumbprint in center.
- Fill center with strawberry preserves.
- Bake at 350 degrees for 12 minutes.

BUTTERSCOTCH OATMEAL COOKIES

1 cup all purpose flour

1 tsp. soda

½ tsp. salt

½ tsp. cinnamon

1 cup butter, softened

¾ cup white granulated sugar

¾ cup brown sugar

2 eggs

1 tsp. vanilla

3 cups oats, uncooked

1 pkg. (12 oz.) butterscotch morsels

Preheat oven to 375 degrees.

- In small bowl, combine flour, soda, salt and cinnamon. Set aside.
- In large bowl combine butter, sugar, brown sugar, eggs and vanilla; beat until light and fluffy.
- Gradually add flour mixture. Stir in oats and morsels.
- Drop by tablespoons on ungreased cookie sheet.
- Bake 7 to 8 minutes for chewier cookies; 9 to 10 minutes for crispy cookies.

*For pan cookies, spread dough into greased 15 x 10 x 1 inch pan. Bake at 375 degrees for 20 to 25 minutes. Cut in squares.

CREAM CHEESE BROWNIES

1 package brownie mix (prepared as directed on package, extra ingredients to prepare brownie mix are probably 1 egg and some cooking oil and water)

2 Tbsp margarine or butter

8 oz. cream cheese

¼ cup sugar

1 egg

1 Tbsp flour

1 tsp. vanilla

- Mix the cream cheese and margarine/butter until blended.
- Add sugar and beat well.
- Blend in egg. Add flour and vanilla and mix well.
- Prepare brownie mix as directed. Pour half of the brownie mixture in ungreased 9x9 pan.
- Evenly spread the cream cheese mixture on top of the brownie mix in the pan.
- Top with spoonfuls of remaining brownie mix and use a spoon to zig-zag through the batter to make a marble effect.
- Bake as directed on brownie mix package.

DREAM BARS

½ cup melted margarine

1 ½ cups graham wafer crumbs

1 (14 ounce) can sweetened condensed milk

1 cup semi-sweet chocolate chips

1 cup flaked coconut

1 cup chopped nuts

- Preheat oven to 350°F.
- In a bowl, mix together margarine and graham wafer crumbs. Press evenly into a lightly greased 13 by 9 inch pan.
- Pour condensed milk over base.
- Working in layers, sprinkle evenly with chocolate chips, then coconut, then nuts. Using a spatula, press down firmly.
- Bake in preheated oven for 25 to 30 minutes or until top is golden.
- Place pan on a rack to cool completely, then cut into bars.

Chapter 9: Pies

If you truly love someone, bake them a pie.

My mother… in addition to milking the cow and raising all our food and sewing our clothes…baked something sweet every day. Yes. You read that correctly. EVERY DAY. Unless there was something sweet left over from the previous day and there was enough of it for all of us. In that case she didn't. But we usually ate it all, so she proceeded to bake. Every Day.

You see, my Daddy loved sweets, especially pies. And my Mama loved my Daddy. She expressed her love every day by baking him a pie.

Occasionally Mama made a cake, but that was less common. Most of the time she baked pies: cream pies, fruit pies, fried pies, cobblers. She made her own pie crusts too.

So, last week when I was craving something sweet, I looked in my cupboard to satisfy that craving. But my cupboard was bare…no store-bought cookies, no Little Debbie snack cakes, not even a cracker fortified with high fructose corn syrup.

But still…there had to be something there. I needed something…something sweet. And so, I reasoned, did my youngest grandchild.

I used my imagination, dug out the family cookbook that my sister compiled for us a few years ago, and decided to make a pie. Yum.

My mother's recipe is for coconut cream pie, but basically any cream pie has the same foundation. As long as you get the cream part down, you can make any kind of pie you want: banana, pineapple (use only canned pineapple), chocolate.

I had nothing but the basic ingredients and some cocoa. Therefore…chocolate cream pie it would be!

Although I didn't have the instructions for how much cocoa to use, I improvised and just added cocoa until I thought it looked right. Life is just one big experiment, after all. Right?

I swear…this pie was so good it made me cry. And it made me miss my Mama. When I fed a few bites of chocolate cream pie to my granddaughter, I could feel my mother close by, smiling at us. I know my grand-baby felt the love there, just as I did.

There's no better way for a proper Southern woman to express her undying love for someone than to bake them a pie. You need to bake one today…and maybe Every Day.

BASIC CREAM PIE

1 cup sugar

3 Tbsp corn starch (or flour)

3 egg yolks

2 cups milk (I used 1 ½ cups of 2 % milk and added a ½ cup of cream)

1 Tbsp vanilla extract

MERINGUE

3 egg whites

¼ teaspoon cream of tartar

¼ cup sugar

1 teaspoon vanilla extract

FOR THE PIE FILLING:

- Slowly heat 1 ½ cups of milk in a 1 ½ or 2 quart sauce pan. Do NOT let it boil.
- Mix sugar and corn starch in a bowl. Set aside.
- In a separate bowl, beat egg yolks well then add ½ cup cold milk. Stir together.
- Add dry ingredients to eggs and milk combination. Mix well. (Should make a nice smooth concoction, like a smoothie)
- Now add the mixture to the hot milk, stirring constantly until it is the consistency of pudding.
- Pour into the baked pie crust.

This makes a cream base. You change the flavor by adding different ingredients to the basic cream recipe.

***Chocolate Cream Pie**: Add ¼ cup cocoa to the sugar and corn starch/flour and mix well. Then add the dry ingredients to the eggs and milk combination.

***Coconut Cream Pie**: Add ½ cup sweetened coconut flakes after cooking to the consistency of pudding. Adjust the amount of coconut to your liking. I love coconut, so I use a lot of it. You can also sprinkle coconut flakes on top of the meringue before baking.

***Pineapple Cream Pie**: Add ½ cup CANNED crushed pineapple after cooking to the consistency of pudding. DO NOT use fresh pineapple because it will make it bitter and inedible.

***Banana Cream Pie**: Add 1 cup banana slices after cooking to the consistency of pudding. Allow pie filling to cool completely before mixing bananas in.

FOR THE MERINGUE TOPPING:

- Add cream of tartar to egg whites. Beat egg whites until very stiff. Add sugar and vanilla, beat until sugar is dissolved.
- (If you don't have cream of tartar, that's OK. My mother never used it and her meringue was excellent…In fact I prefer not to use cream of tartar because I like the meringue better without it.)
- Spread egg whites on pie and brown in 350 degree oven…10 minutes maybe…possibly more…depends on how brown you like your meringue. It doesn't take long, so don't walk out of the kitchen and forget you've got something in the oven! (Don't laugh. It happens.)

BUTTERMILK CHESS PIE

3 eggs

1 ½ cups sugar

2 Tbsp flour

1 stick oleo or butter

1 cup buttermilk

1 tsp. vanilla

- Melt butter; let it cool slightly.
- Beat eggs and sugar until light and fluffy.
- Add cooled melted butter, buttermilk, flour, and vanilla to the egg and sugar mixture.
- Pour into an uncooked pie shell. Bake at 350 degrees (F) about 1 hour or until firm.

PECAN PIE

1 cup Karo corn syrup (light or dark, it doesn't matter)

1 cup sugar

3 eggs, beaten

½ tsp. vanilla

1 cup pecans

- Beat eggs until frothy.
- Mix all ingredients together and pour into unbaked pie crust.
- Bake 1 hour at 350 degrees.

Yes… it really is that easy

PINEAPPLE CHESS PIE

2 cups sugar

½ cup butter

4 egg yolks

2 Tbsp flour

4 egg whites

1 cup crushed, canned pineapple (canned, crushed)

*Do NOT use fresh pineapple for this recipe.

- Drain pineapple juice.
- Separate egg whites from yolks.
- Set aside egg whites. Beat egg yolks.
- Cream butter, sugar and flour together.
- Add beaten egg yolks.
- Beat egg whites until stiff. Then gently fold pineapple and egg whites into butter and egg mixture.
- Place in unbaked pie crust.
- Bake at 325 degrees for approximately 1 hour or until a knife inserted in middle comes out clean.

EAGLE BRAND LEMON PIE

1 can sweetened condensed milk

¼ cup lemon juice

2 egg yolks

¼ tsp. vanilla

- Combine milk and egg yolks. Blend well.
- Blend in lemon juice and vanilla.
- Stir until it thickens.
- After it thickens, pour in baked Graham Cracker Crust.

MERINGUE

- Beat egg whites until stiff, add ¼ cup sugar and ¼ tsp. vanilla.
- Top pie with meringue mixture and bake at 350 degrees until meringue is lightly browned.

CHERRY CREAM CHEESE PIE

1 (8 oz.) package cream cheese, softened

1 (14 oz.) can sweetened condensed milk

1/3 cup lemon juice

1 teaspoon vanilla extract

1 (8 or 9-inch) prepared graham cracker or baked pie crust

1 (21 oz.) can cherry pie filling, chilled

- Beat cream cheese until fluffy in large bowl. Gradually beat in sweetened condensed milk until smooth. Stir in lemon juice and vanilla.

- Pour into crust; chill 4 hours or until set. Top with desired amount of cherry pie filling before serving.

***You can vary the toppings by changing the ingredients somewhat. Here are some suggestions:**

Blueberry: Combine ¼ cup sugar and 1 tablespoon cornstarch in medium bowl; mix well. Add ½ cup water, 2 tablespoons lemon juice then 2 cup fresh or frozen unsweetened blueberries; mix well. Bring to a boil; reduce heat and simmer 3 minutes or until thick and clear. Cool 10 minutes, stirring constantly. Cool 15 minutes. Spread over pie. Chill thoroughly.

Cranberry: Combine 1/3 cups sugar and 1 tablespoon cornstarch in medium saucepan. Add ½ cup plus 2 tablespoons cold water and 2 cups fresh or frozen cranberries; mix well. Bring to a boil; reduce heat and simmer 10 minutes. Cool 15 minutes. Spread over pie. Chill thoroughly.

Fresh Fruit: Just before serving, arrange well-drained fresh strawberries, banana slices (dipped in lemon juice and well drained) and blueberries on top of chilled pie. Brush fruit with light corn syrup if desired.

Ambrosia: Combine ½ cup peach or apricot preserves, ¼ cup flaked coconut, 2 tablespoons orange juice and 2 teaspoons cornstarch in small saucepan; cook and stir until thickened. Remove from heat. Arrange fresh orange sections over top of pie; top with coconut mixture. Chill thoroughly.

NOTES:

***Note: with the exception of Graham Cracker Pie Crust, I do not make my own pie crusts. Pillsbury does a much better job than I do of making pie crusts. The crusts are available in the dairy section beside cans of cinnamon rolls and biscuits.**

GRAHAM CRACKER PIE CRUST

Place 1 pack of fresh graham crackers in a plastic bag.

Using rolling pin to crush the graham crackers into fine crumbs.

Combine crumbs, ¼ cup granulated sugar, and 1/3 cup softened butter or margarine.

Blend well with a fork or pastry blender.

When crumbs, butter, and sugar are blended, pour them in a 9 inch pie pan.

Use the back of a large spoon to spread and press the mixture evenly on to the bottom and sides of the pan.

FOR BAKED CRUST:

Bake at 375 degrees (F) for 8 minutes. Cool before placing pie ingredients in it.

FOR NO-BAKE CRUST:

Chill in refrigerator for at least 30 minutes before using. Fill with your favorite chilled pie filling.

Index: Abbreviations & Measurements

Teaspoon - tsp.

Tablespoon - Tbsp

Ounce - oz.

Pound - lb.

Gallon – gal.

Pint - pt.

Quart – qt.

Cup – cup or c.

Package – pkg.

Fahrenheit – F or Fahrenheit

*All recipes use American measurements.

Acknowledgments:

This is from the grammarphobia blog, written by Patricia T. O'Conner and Stewart Kellerman.

Is the cheese blue or bleu?

DECEMBER 23RD, 2013

Q: I was always a snob and looked down on the poor souls who referred to "bleu cheese" as "blue cheese." Now "blue" seems to be the preferred spelling. Did this misspelling become acceptable because "bleu" *seemed* like a mistake to most Americans?

A: You'll be dismayed to hear this, but the phrase "blue cheese" showed up in English a century and a half before the Frenchified "bleu cheese" version.

In fact, the phrase "blue cheese" may have appeared in English before *fromage bleu* made its appearance in French. Here's the story.

The earliest example of the phrase "blue cheese" in the *Oxford English Dictionary* is from an Aug. 3, 1787, entry in *The Torrington Diaries*, an account of John Byng Torrington's travels in England and Wales:

"I eat to day at dinner, and at supper, some excellent blue cheese … which … resembles, both in color and taste, the blue mold of Cheshire cheese."

From Grammarphobia blog by Patricia T. O'Conner and Stewart Kellerman

www.grammarphobia.com

Photographs:

Pages 3, 7,17,13,47,48,67,110, 118, 127 from author's personal collection.

Page 1 foto76/freedigitalphotos.net

Page 18 & 37 apolonia/freedigitalphotos.net

Page 39 tiverylucky/freedigitalphotos.net

Page 41 khunaspix/freedigitalphotos.net

Page 47 tiramisustudio/freedigitalphotos.net

Page 59 Super trooper/freedigitalphotos.net

Page 61 radnatt/freedigitalphotos.net

Page 73 anankml/freedigitalphotos.net

Page 83 phasinphoto/freedigitalphotos.net

Page 103 Viaschler Blixniak/freedigitalphotos.net

Page 109 Mr GC/freedigitalphotos.net

Page 133 Tina Phillips/freedigitalphotos.net

Thank you for buying and reading this book. I hope you enjoy the recipes here and that you make memories that feed your heart and soul and family well.
Peggy Browning

ABOUT THE AUTHOR

Peggy Browning is author of several books including The View Through My Rose-Colored Bifocals; Well Seasoned: A Year of Living, Laughing, Loving; Square Peg's Words of Wisdom.
She also writes as Elaine Jewel.

www.ingramcontent.com/pod-product-compliance
Lightning Source LLC
LaVergne TN
LVHW030912080826
845145LV00010B/2864

* 9 7 8 1 9 5 4 3 4 3 1 2 2 *